I don't
mean
to be
rude,
but...

I don't mean

to be

Backstage Gossip From

AMERICAN IDOL

& the Secrets That Can
Make You A STAR

BROADWAY BOOKS

New York

rude,
but...

SIMON * COWELL

PRINTED IN THE UNITED STATES OF AMERICA

BROADWAY BOOKS and its logo, a letter B bisected on the diagonal, are trademarks of Random House, Inc.

Visit our website at www.broadwaybooks.com.

First edition published 2003.

Designed by Erin L. Matherne and Tina Thompson

Cataloging-in-Publication Data is on file with the Library of Congress.

ISBN 0-7679-1741-3

10 9 8 7 6 5 4 3 2 1

Dedicated to my father, Eric Cowell

Contents

Introduction

Just like thirty-eight million other people, I was watching when Ruben Studdard was crowned as the second American Idol in June of 2003. The only difference is that I was ten yards away from Ruben rather than miles away, watching him in person rather than on television. And there's also the small fact of what the selection meant to me. I didn't care if Ruben won or if Clay won; I didn't care a bit. But the fact that so many people were voting to make the selection meant the world to me, because it proved me right. I had been part of *American Idol* since before anyone had heard of Ruben or Clay, or Kelly or Justin, or Paula and Randy.

So maybe I wasn't just like those thirty-eight million other people. Maybe I was a little different.

I don't mean to be rude, but . . . since the birth of *American Idol,* people have expected nothing less of me. You see, I have become famous for being rude. At first, I was "the British one," but in short order I became "the obnoxious one," "the opinionated one," or "the brutal one." Well, in my mind, I'm the honest one. That's all. On *American Idol,* I have only ever said whatever I'm thinking at the time. That's the only way I can describe what I'm doing. My statements are genuine. Nothing is rehearsed. When a woman walks in to audition, I might think, "God, she's ugly." And this, as luck would have it, is the one show on television where I can actually say, "God, you're ugly." Since the show's rise to popularity in America, I have witnessed a strange phenomenon: In the street, people will come up to me and say "Will you criticize me?" Apparently, it's a strange badge of honor to be insulted by me. It seems like a masochistic pastime, frankly, but I'm happy to oblige.

The tone of my comments is part of the entertainment. Without it, *American Idol* wouldn't be half as much fun, either for me or for the viewers. But there's a subtler point behind my honesty—or, if you must be so thin-skinned, my rudeness. The music industry is a culture awash with sycophants and yes-men. There's far too much decorum and protocol. I can't see the point of that. When it comes down to it, the industry should do only one thing: find out who is really marketable and why. The rest is wasted time and wasted breath. And today, the record business is harder to break into than ever before. Labels are less willing to invest money in a new artist unless they have something really special to offer—like Justin Timberlake, whose romantic relationship with Britney Spears guaranteed loads of publicity and a surefire road to fame. That's why I prefer to cut through the white lies and the bullshit. My harsh criticism may be tough on some people, but in the main it tends to have a positive effect. Once the initial shock passes, people want to know how they're perceived by an audience, and especially a member of the audience who is experienced, articulate, and able to understand what might improve that perception. Most important, it separates the wannabes from the real stars, and does so as swiftly and uncomfortably as possible. We set out to make a show that honestly reflects the music business. And trust me—the record industry is *not* nice.

If you have bought this book, you are probably already familiar with my personality and the fact that it gets results. I have made millions from taking beginners with raw talent and, through coaching and brutal honesty, turning those hopefuls into global pop stars. With this book, you'll be able to start the difficult but rewarding process of ascertaining whether or not you're one of the lucky few who can make it.

Part of this book is my story. It has to be: For starters, I'm very interesting, and I'm enough of an egotist to be honest about that. My story has lessons for anyone who sets his or her eye on fame. I'll take you behind the scenes of the music industry and give you the real scoop on what it takes to make it to the top, based on my own career and on the careers that I have guided. Because I'm the ultimate insider on *American Idol,* I'll be able to tell you the real truth about what happens backstage on the show: about the rivalries and the alliances; about the image makeovers that worked and the ones that didn't (does anyone remember—shudder—Clay Aiken in leather?); about me and Paula Abdul. But mainly about me.

Most importantly, I'll share some secrets with you about talent, about how to recognize it and cultivate it. You'll learn how to develop your skills—assuming you have any to begin with—and how to handle an audition and stand out from the crowd. And I won't hold back when it comes to established pop stars: Some of them are falling fast, and I'll say so; I'll also explain which ones I'd send packing if they auditioned for *American Idol.* There isn't any substitute for talent, unless of course you have a famous dad like Julio Iglesias, in which case it doesn't matter that you can't sing a note. But even if you have all the talent in the world—and almost no one does—you can't make it to the top without the right guidance. By "the right guidance," of course, I mean my guidance.

Let me explain with a short example. Back in the early nineties, I set my sights on signing Robson Green and Jerome Flynn, two relatively unknown actors from a successful British TV series called *Soldier Soldier.* My reasoning was pretty straightforward: They were good-looking, they could sing (a bit), and they had already built up an enormous female fan base from their television show. I phoned them three times a day, every day, for seven months, saying that I would guarantee them a number-one hit if they would record a song with me. They consistently ignored my advances—until, that is, I offered them a six-figure sum that they could keep whether they had a hit record or not. Not surprisingly, they accepted my offer. Robson and Jerome's first single was a remake of the classic Righteous Brothers song "Unchained Melody." It sold over two million copies in the first two weeks of its release and went on to become the U.K.'s biggest-selling single of the 1990s. That was followed by two more number-one singles and two number-one albums, and by the time Robson and Jerome returned to their acting careers two years later, they were multimillionaires.

People like Paula Abdul and Randy Jackson like to talk about the importance of self-confidence. Believe in yourself, they'll say ad nauseam—especially if they're making a promotional appearance on *Oprah*. I won't deny that confidence is an important part of stardom. But I believe in something even more important—what I call the X Factor. This is that indefinable quality that sets you apart from other ambitious young people, some of whom can sing, some of whom can dance, and all of whom want to see their name in lights. The X Factor draws people to you and translates to real star power. It's also somewhat beyond your control. Madonna had it, of course, and all the American Idols—Kelly Clarkson, Ruben Studdard, and Clay Aiken—have had it. Even though each developed as a talent and gained more confidence as the show progressed, they all

I DON'T MEAN TO BE RUDE, BUT . . .
Madonna's Over

If you're looking for a blueprint for stardom that includes all the ingredients—self-confidence, talent and naked ambition—you don't have to look any further than Madonna. The young Madonna, that is, the Madonna of the early eighties. When she exploded onto the music scene, she could sing and dance just fine, but that wasn't what made her a megastar. In addition to talent, she had an innate ability to know exactly what the market and the media wanted: sex. She possessed it, and she knew how to make everyone else feel like they could almost, but not quite, possess it. It was a tease that was also completely satisfying, and it was a brilliant career. From an insider's point of view, Madonna's approach was interesting. She ignored the tradi-tional approach, which was to work through record companies, and instead decided to take an alternative route. She went directly to the top record producer, Jelly Bean Benitez, who skill-fully honed her first hit single, "Holiday." Then, armed with a highly polished product, they approached Sire Records and struck a deal. The rest, as they say, is history. Today, though, the Madonna of that era is no more. Ten to fifteen years ago, I could hum along to 90 percent of her music. Now I can't. And while she used to be a genius of the provocative gesture, now she goes in for bizarrely awful theatre like that kiss with Britney Spears at the MTV Awards, which, to me, was the equivalent of my mother getting drunk at a wedding and then trying to kiss the groom to get noticed. If Madonna really believed that kissing the semivirginal Britney Spears would increase record sales, she's insane. The problem with her, I think, is that she is addicted to fame as badly as a junkie is to any drug. When she was young, she wanted fame more than anyone on earth, and now she doesn't want to give it up. The kiss, the ghastly Gap advert—it all seems desperate. And, worst of all, embarrassing.

---

possessed an innate charisma that drew the audience to them the minute they started singing. What I hope for during the audition process of *American Idol* is to find that one person who has the X Factor, and then to help guide them to great stardom. I'm sure that I can do it, and I'm sure that if the show casts a wide enough net, we can find that person. But the X Factor is also vital to anyone who aspires to stardom. You either have it or you don't, and you're not going to be the one who is able to determine that. Someone else has to tell you—someone candid, someone unsparing, and maybe someone British. Self-knowledge is far more important than self-confidence.

When I was initially offered the chance to be a judge on the first *American Idol,* I actually turned it down. I helped develop the concept in Britain, where it was called *Pop Idol,* but I figured that the national difference was everything. I was British, and I felt that Americans would never want a British guy to sit there and pass judgment on American talent. Everyone thought I was mad to turn down such an opportunity. In the end, I recanted and decided to judge. Maybe the amount of money had something to do with it, but I also came to the realization that it didn't matter a fig if I was British. Even before *Pop Idol* I had been judging talent for more than twenty-five years. The bands I produced had sold more than ninety million records. Clearly there was no one better suited to judge *American Idol* than me. See, there I go, doing exactly what Randy and Paula said I should do. I'm believing in myself.

Believing in yourself, though, sometimes means shutting out what others say about you. Many celebrities make the fatal mistake of reading their press, absorbing it, and then starting to shift their own ideas about themselves on the basis of what fans and critics say about them. Michael Jackson, if you're reading this book, I'm talking about you. But I'm also talking about me, to some degree. About a month into the first season of *American Idol*, I found that I was a celebrity in ways that I could never have predicted. I was invited onto *The Tonight Show with Jay Leno*. I did the Letterman show. Wherever I went, I was instantly recognized and mobbed by people.

Then, partly because I was curious and partly because I am an eternal egotist, I made the mistake of logging on to the *American Idol* Web site and going to the Judges section, where fans can leave messages for us. I was absolutely horrified. There were hundreds of nasty comments about me. I began searching desperately to see if anyone had anything *nice* to say about me. They didn't. It was as if I were reading about Leona Helmsley, or Pol Pot, or any other of history's great monsters. The more I read, the more I began to believe the terrible things that people were saying. Here are a few examples of the nasty comments from the Web site:

To say Simon is just plain mean is an understatement. I think he's mean, brutal, totally ruthless, and a complete pain in the ass. He's rude, arrogant, and way over the top. Let's write to Fox and have him deported back to England.

Hey—you all—why is Simon Cowell so sarcastic and degrading to just about every contestant on the show? Is he really like this in real life? If American Idol is supposed to be reality TV, then maybe he needs to give *himself* a reality check—his comments just stink.

Simon—you are the most egotistical, rude, and bad mannered Brit I have ever heard. Every week you insult the cream of America's home-grown talent. You need to go back to Britain and get a brain scan because you don't know a good singer when you hear one. I hope that someday one of the contestants physically attacks you.

And people say *I'm* rude.

The next week on the show, I realized that these comments were starting to influence the way I was behaving. In short, I was behaving. I was observing myself at a distance, trying to be more judicious than usual, even saying kind things that I didn't exactly mean, but that I rationalized as important to building the confidence of these budding young entertainers. At one point I found myself agreeing with Paula. That was the last straw. In my eagerness to offset some of the dreadful comments, I had lost the edge that made the show work. There is a lesson here for all of you—especially you, Ryan Seacrest. You can believe in yourself, but that doesn't mean persisting with an unrealistic view of your talents.

At the same time, it doesn't mean letting the unwarranted opinions of others change your course. (This may sound hypocritical, especially for someone who is probably best known for delivering opinions of others, but it's important to see the distinction between my weekly comments on the show and the moaning of a few disgruntled viewers. The key, as I have said, is *unwarranted* opinions. And when it comes to judging talent, at least, I'm always right.)

In today's celebrity-obsessed world, every youngster wants to be famous. Who wouldn't? The crazy excesses of stars like J.Lo and P. Diddy make for fascinating reading and inspire thousands of would-be pop stars to run out and hire a voice coach. J.Lo, in particular, embodies the American Dream: Her rags-to-riches story proves that anyone can do great things with hard work, talent, and a little luck. With charisma, charm, and that elusive X Factor, J.Lo has been able to achieve unparalleled success in both her singing and acting careers (*Gigli* aside). And anyone who can make light of herself by saying, "You can serve coffee using my rear as a ledge" is fine by me. If you are an aspiring P. Diddy, however, you should remember that you won't just have to buy nice suits. You'll also have to see to it that your initials are sewn onto every sheet, pillowcase, and white suede chair that adorns your home. Sad.

All joking aside, the problem is that most people don't understand that to be successful in the music business you have to first have talent. It's not enough to come to an audition with stars in your eyes, dreamily contemplating your own inevitable rise to fame. It's not enough to come to an audition with a costume or an attitude. People will do the strangest things just to hide the fact they are completely and utterly talentless.

Before the first season of *American Idol* ever aired, we came to New York for auditions, and the first person through the door introduced himself as "Milk." The second I heard that name, I thought to myself, "Okay, we may have a problem here." Then there was the fact that he looked like Clark Kent, if Clark Kent had been stupid enough to wear a bandanna around his head. First impressions count in this business: You can either confirm them or contradict them, but they count. In this case, he confirmed them, with spectacular incompetence. He sang, or tried to sing, a version of Neil Diamond's "Sweet Caroline" interspersed with Vietnamese war footage that he acted out—or rather, overacted out. When he was finished, I turned to Randy and said, "What do you think?"

"Well, I'm not sure," Randy said.

Not sure? How could he not be sure? I was so mad that I thought about standing up, walking out, and letting Randy judge the competition on his own. It was obvious to anyone with half a brain that the guy was terrible, just awful, and he needed to be told as much. So I told him.

In the second season, during the Austin, Texas, auditions, some other idiot walked in wearing a yellow suit. He looked like a gigantic banana—and, like a gigantic banana, he couldn't sing a note. He was followed by a guy dressed as a lizard. For future reference, I want to tell all aspiring American Idols this: If you can't sing, don't come to the audition. No matter what you're wearing, I'll see through it. (Later that same week, we had a girl who plugged herself into a wall so she lit up like a Christmas tree when she sang. Or rather, tried to sing. On the whole, I was rather disappointed with the talent in Austin.)

The music business is like football. Everyone wants to be as good as the Super Bowl champs, whoever they are. (Not that I know much about American football, but there must be some team that's better than all the others.) But there is a huge difference between playing for your high school team and playing for the Super Bowl champs. Likewise, there is a big difference between singing along with your guitar in your garage and selling five million albums a year. The problem is that too many people think that they're capable of playing quarterback in the Super Bowl, and they're dead wrong.

Let's go back to the X Factor for a moment. Even if you have a voice like Barbra Streisand, you won't get very far if you're essentially unappealing. All the biggest pop stars, from Elvis and the Beatles to Elton John and Madonna, have possessed that elusive X Factor. Frank Sinatra wasn't the best singer, technically—there were others with better pitch and range—but he had an aura. When he walked onstage and tilted his head up toward the microphone, you were transfixed. He had such stage presence. He was a born star. So what is it that made these artists so successful? What has helped them sustain their popularity? What set them apart from the wannabes of their time? And why am I the only man on earth who can explain it all to you?

Keep reading.

The Birth
of the Rude

The first time I was rude to someone I was four years old.
Unfortunately, my mum was the victim. It was December 1963,
less than a month after President Kennedy had been assassi-
nated. In London, this tragic event had an enormous impact.
The British government was still reeling from the Profumo call-
girl scandal, in which top government officials, including John
Profumo, the Minister of War, were caught with their pants down.
The country's newly elected Prime Minister, Alec Douglas-
Home, was only a month into his tenure. He didn't last long
after that; he was an idiot.

The mood at home was particularly glum. Dad was a
staunch Conservative, and had it not been for his success as a

property agent, he might have gone into politics. As a result, the upheaval in the political world, both at home and in America, upset him greatly. Still, he made it clear to the rest of the family that it was essential, if only for the sake of the children, to continue with our plans for Christmas. This came as a blessed relief to me—the thought that anything could possibly hijack my Christmas toy delivery was my first and only concern.

On Christmas Day, Mum was seated in her vast mirrored dressing room, putting the final touches on her makeup. As a young girl, she had studied ballet and idolized the famous British dancer Dame Margot Fonteyn; when she met and married my father, she was working as a dancer in the London theatre. With her dark, sultry looks, Mum radiated charm and sophistication, and was often compared to a young Liz Taylor in her *National Velvet* days. But like many women in Britain at that time, she modeled herself on that quintessential icon of style, Jackie Kennedy. Mum had it down to a fine art: She had the same trim figure, the same raven hair, the same cropped suit and pillbox hats. That night, the crowning glory of her movie-star outfit was a huge white mink hat.

I was crouching at the foot of the stairs with my new train set. The one highlight of an otherwise dull collection of Christmas presents, it was spread before me on the vast wood floor as Mum made her entrance down the sweeping grand staircase.

"What do you think, darling?" she asked, stepping cautiously over the railway track. "Does Mummy look pretty?"

I looked up at her and stared at the furry hat. "Mum," I said, "you look like a poodle."

I was born in October 1959, into postwar Britain, and grew up in a sizable home on a small estate in Elstree, north of London. My father was a prosperous real-estate developer, my mother was something of a local socialite, and my brothers—Michael, who was thirteen years older than me; Tony, who was nine years older; and Nicholas, who was eighteen months younger—were, well, my brothers. We played, we fought, we terrorized each other and the house staff. More on that later. The world I was born into was very different than the world is now: We had no McDonald's, no color television, and luckily no Paula Abdul.

The fifties had been an austere period in Britain—lots of belt-tightening after the war, and lots of gray predictions about the economy and the culture. As the sixties dawned, it was the first time teenagers could get decent work and the chance to earn some money. Better still, they could hang on to their teenage dreams, which for many meant forming a pop group. And not an old-style pop group, with barbershop singing. In Britain in the sixties, we grew up with proper rock-and-roll groups, smack-dab in the middle of the biggest music revolution the world has ever known.

My early childhood was accompanied by a soundtrack of some of the most exciting music ever produced. Elvis was one of the first rock-and-roll singers I ever heard. The British press at the time referred to him as "an American teenager throb-bing with sex." And it wasn't only kids that loved Elvis, their mums did, too! Elvis and his management team, including the legendary Colonel Tom Parker, were the first to recognize television as the most powerful method of selling millions of records.

A little later my elder brother, Tony, bought the first Bob Dylan album, which he proceeded to play over and over again while struggling to sing along in Dylan's nasal vocal style. I'm not sure who sounded worse. Today, neither my brother nor Bob Dylan would get through a single audition on *American Idol*—at least as long as I remain one of the judges. One of them can't sing and the other's too earnest and boring. Throughout this era of early rock-and-roll, my parents continued their long-running affair with artists such as Frank Sinatra and Tony Bennett. As a child, these artists did nothing for me—though I eventually came to understand the appeal of Sinatra as an entertainer and stage presence.

And then, of course, the Beatles came onto the music scene and changed it in ways that no one could have predicted. At the end of 1963—during the same dismal period I mentioned earlier, when the Kennedy assassination was on everyone's mind—the Beatles had hit number one on the pop charts with "She Loves You," which was also the first record I can remember asking my mum to buy for me. In part, this was because my elder brother, Tony, had it, but it wasn't only a matter of imitation. It was the first time in my life that I had been interested in music; and I was desperate to own a copy. There was something about that music that made me sit up and listen.

For a while there in my youth, the Beatles were everything to everyone. They were bigger than politics, bigger than religion, bigger than national identity. The Beatles were the first real rock group and the first boy band. Up to then, British kids had existed on a diet of American rock stars like Elvis, Little Richard, Jerry Lee Lewis, and somewhat less revolutionary homegrown singers like Cliff Richard and Adam Faith. The birth of the Beatles came like a bolt out of the blue. Their sound was just *so* different.

At the time, it seemed like a wonderful, peaceful revolution. What I didn't realize then—I was only five years old, after all—is that record companies were the main benefactors of the Beatles' ascendancy. Soon, the British public was bombarded by sound-alike bands like the Hollies and the Dave Clark Five, looking to jump on the bandwagon. The cultural revolution meant big money for someone. And after *Time* magazine coined the phrase "Swinging London," it was only a matter of time before America got the message, too. The next Beatles record, "I Want to Hold Your Hand," went to number one in the United States and four Beatles tracks went simultaneously into the top five slots on the *Billboard* charts.

Rehashing the Beatles' early career may sound like ancient history, in a sense, but it's also important history, because it utterly changed the possibilities for popular entertainers. Not only were the Beatles wonderful singers and increasingly talented songwriters, but they were something else: celebrities at a level for which there was no precedent. The Beatles were also the first band to be photographed living it up in what we now perceive as traditional rock-star fashion. They were seen lounging in the backs of limos, drinking champagne, and lording it up in hotel suites. But they were also young and boyish and seemed utterly distinct from the musical acts of previous generations. For the first time young people looked at them and thought wistfully, "That could be me."

I was one of those young people.

I spent my happy childhood, as I have said, growing up in a large country house in Elstree, a small town just twenty miles north of London. Abbots Mead, the house, was on five acres of landscaped grounds. Most country houses in England have grand names; as this particular grand name suggests, Abbots Mead was originally used as a retreat for monks and friars. My father, Eric, was a quantity surveyor. His job involved assessing a building site and determining the materials necessary for completing the construction, and he had purchased Abbots Mead as a sad ruin. Convinced he could return the house to its former glory, he spent two years gutting and then rebuilding the interior. The house itself was built on four floors with eight bedrooms, four bathrooms, and a host of nooks and crannies in which to hide and explore. For a naughty four-year-old boy, Abbots Mead was the perfect place in which to grow up.

Life at home was a well-organized affair. Mum was the captain, and she ran a tight and orderly ship. We had a gardener named Robin who pruned and tended the gardens. Mrs. Ostler cleaned the house and kept it shipshape. And Heather, our devoted live-in nanny, had perhaps the hardest job of anyone. Heather looked after the three Cowell children: Tony, Nicholas, and me. If we were little devils, Heather was nothing less than an angel. She cooked for us, cleaned for us, and even made sure Tony was in bed before two in the morning—he was just entering his trainee rock-star rebellion period, and didn't care for rules and regulations. To this day, she still has a number of mementos from her years with us, including my old pink-colored pram, which she proudly displayed on British TV this past year. Thanks, Heather!

In those days, Elstree was the Hollywood of the British film industry. It had begun as a sleepy country village, but then, in the early part of the century, two major studios were built there and a town grew up around them and the jobs. Those two studios, MGM and Associated British Picture Corporation, were the home for a string of classic British films, including *Secret Ceremony* with Elizabeth Taylor, *Where Eagles Dare* with Richard Burton, Sam Peckinpah's *The Dirty Dozen*, and Stanley Kubrick's *2001: A Space Odyssey*. In fact, some years later, Kubrick himself bought Abbots Mead from my parents. According to my dad—who had always been a snob when it came to architecture and interior design—Kubrick ruined the house by turning most of the ground floor into a private cinema.

During my childhood, the stars who worked at Elstree included Roger Moore, Gregory Peck, Robert Mitchum, Bette

Davis, and Maureen O'Hara. This created a brand-new world of celebrity for my parents—and, by extension, for me. The stars soon became our friends and neighbors, and whenever they were in town I got to rub shoulders with the cream of Hollywood, as long as I could squeeze my way past my mum. The leader of this exclusive Hollywood circle was our closest neighbor, Gerry Blatner. Gerry was head of Warner Brothers Films in the U.K., and whenever Hollywood stars came to Elstree they would stay at Gerry's house. The first guest of Gerry's that Mum ever met (over the garden fence) was Bette Davis, who became a regular visitor to the house. There are not many kids who can say that they sat on the knee of Bette Davis while she learned her lines. (Though how she managed to learn her lines at all in the presence of my mum, who could outtalk anyone, remains a complete mystery.)

Roger Moore, best known as James Bond, was another star who was in town quite often. Mum was a big fan of his television show *The Saint,* which had rocketed him to fame, and Roger would often invite us to watch him film the TV show on the back lot of Elstree Studios. By this time Tony was working as a runner on the show, and his job was to drive and position the cars on the set. Often he would let me ride around the studios in the back seat while he drove, as long as I kept my head down—which, of course, I stubbornly refused to do. Other frequent dinner guests were British actor Trevor Howard and his wife, Helen Cherry. Trevor once asked me if I wanted to be an actor when I grew up. "No," I replied curtly. "I don't like actors."

With Mum so at home with "theatrical" types—it came from her days on the London stage, she always said—it wasn't long before the Cowell family was enjoying a nonstop whirl of film industry parties, often held at Abbots Mead. My parents entertained with endless cocktail hours and formal dinners. From my perch at the top of the staircase, I often peeked through the rails in fascination at the scantily dressed women sipping champagne. This is an interest, I admit, I have never lost.

Some nights, as the music and laughter increased, I would venture farther down the staircase, step by step. I knew that if I attracted the attention of one of the more intoxicated guests I would soon be invited down to join the fun. My dad cut a handsome figure. In fact, with his jet-black hair and stylish suits, he was often mistaken for one of Gerry Blatner's film-star guests. Dad had a wicked sense of humor and would hold court at dinner parties with a nonstop stream of witty anecdotes and rude stories, which he delivered with a deadpan face.

Dad was highly successful in his business and worked hard to make his money. That meant, of course, that he was off to work early each day; every morning at 7:30 A.M. he would jump into his white E Type Jaguar and drive the twenty miles to his London office with the hood down and one of his trademark Cuban cigars in his mouth. With Dad away most of the day, the bulk of our rearing was left to Mum. And since my own disobedient tendencies were apparent from an early age, that meant that Mum had to take a firm hand with me. She was always telling me what to do or what not to do, and I was forever refusing to listen to her.

It is easy, with hindsight, to reflect on how this privileged upbringing and artistically rich atmosphere came to influence my love of music and films. It certainly gave me confidence at a very early age. I was perfectly at home in these glamorous worlds. Mixing with the Hollywood elite, I always had a feeling that I would someday end up working in the entertainment business.

While the Beatles and the Rolling Stones dominated the British radio airwaves during the mid-sixties, my parents hadn't really noticed. The dulcet tones that reverberated down the corridors of Abbots Mead, mostly in the early hours of the morning, belonged exclusively to (yawn) Frank Sinatra, Shirley Bassey, Perry Como, and Jack Jones (Mum had the hots for Jack). They were all hugely successful artists, but to a four-year-old, strong-willed little boy, not to mention his teenage older brother, they were nothing short of terrible noise. I would have rather listened to Tony, drunk on Dad's beer and trying to play his guitar, than endure anything by Perry Como. I may not have been able to read, but I already knew precisely what music I *didn't* like—and my parents had a sizable collection of it. I would constantly beg Mum to "turn that rubbish off," and I even began to hide the records I hated most by slipping them under the expansive sofas in the lounge. One day in a fit of pique I actually put a huge scratch across one of Mum's favorite records using one of Dad's screwdrivers. I was determined that I would never have to hear Shirley Bassey ever again.

Tony had been banished to the top floor of the house, as he was in his early teens. It was there, in Tony's smoky bedroom, that I first experienced a wide range of rock and pop stars—Bob Dylan, Neil Young, the Beach Boys, and even Tom Jones—and listened to Tony's own painfully pathetic attempts to emulate Jimi Hendrix. It's such a shame I was too young to offer him my informed opinion and guidance.

But my first music lesson at school gave me just that opportunity. As a five-year-old in a rowdy class of twenty other junior Beatles, I was anxious to get my hands on a guitar like Tony's. My po-faced music teacher, Mrs. Jones, had other ideas. She made me play the bass drum. Not at all amused by the choice of instrument, I proceeded to bang the drum so hard that it drowned everyone else out. Mrs. Jones looked on in horror and promptly swapped my drum for a triangle in a vain attempt to bring some order to the class. I soon realized what a complete and utter racket we were making; it was terrible. I raised my hand and demanded an explanation. "Miss," I said, "this is absolutely dreadful. Why are you making us do it?"

I had no idea back then that this was how I would end up making millions.

Neither did Mrs. Jones, who saw to it that I was promptly escorted out of the class and not allowed back. Thank God.

———

At home I was, like many boys, something of a brat, especially to my younger brother, Nicholas. While I idolized Tony—he was so much older that he seemed to come from another world—Nicholas was only a year and a half younger, which meant that he was almost a kind of twin. This also meant that he was the competition. Before he appeared on the scene, I had been the star. So my main goal, from the time he could walk, was to get him into as much trouble as possible. Luckily for me, Nicholas was more than willing. I soon realized that all the naughty things I wanted to do I could get Nicholas to do for me—and also take the blame. Perfect.

Some of the mischief that I remember revolved around Santa Claus. One Christmas Eve, I spotted Dad creeping into our bedroom laden down with sacks full of presents. I had been a cynic since I was seven or so, and I was pretty certain that Santa Claus was just a story adults told to gullible children. When I saw Dad, I knew that I was right, and as soon as he had left the room, I immediately woke Nicholas and spilled the beans. "Santa isn't real," I said, "and the quicker you come to terms with it, the better." He was in tears and wouldn't believe what I was saying.

The following Christmas, I gleefully took a huge collection of pots and pans from the kitchen and balanced them carefully along the top of our bedroom door. Later that night, when Dad crept in with our toy delivery, there was an enormous crash as the kitchenware came raining down on him. Nicholas shot bolt upright in bed and glared at Dad. I turned to Nicholas with a big grin on my face and proudly announced, "See, I told you, Santa Claus does not exist." Nicholas burst into tears, and Dad looked sheepish as he left the room, kicking out at the pots and pans that littered the bedroom floor.

Weeks later, to my delight, I discovered Dad's Santa Claus suit hidden in the attic. I couldn't wait to show my little brother. He was devastated. "Is Santa dead?" he asked.

"Don't be stupid," I replied sharply. "He was never alive." I couldn't believe he was taking so long to get the message. To drive home the point, I suggested that we should set fire to Santa's beard. At first Nicholas didn't want to do it.

"Why should I?" he whined.

"Because Simon says," I replied with confidence.

We torched the suit. It began to crackle, and we giggled as thick smoke filled the attic.

Tony was sixteen at the time, and he was supposed to be keeping an eye on the two of us. He smelled the burning suit and came running up the stairs in a panic. He managed to extinguish the fire and was able to save Santa's torso, but sadly not his legs. At least, as we told Mum, the house didn't burn down.

Nicholas was such a willing apprentice that he became a kind of test pilot for all my schemes. One day I decided that he needed a haircut and that I would be the one to give it to him. It was my first attempt at an image makeover. I sat him on a stool in the middle of his bedroom and pulled a big pair of scissors from the drawer. I said, "Nicholas—that hair has to go," and proceeded to chop off great chunks of his hair till the floor was covered with his thick, dark locks. He looked like a mad monk, his scalp peeking through on the top.

Once I had completed his makeover, Nicholas couldn't wait to go downstairs and show off his new style to Mum. I shall never forget the tone of Mum's voice as it thundered through the house: *"WHERE . . . IS . . . SIMON?"*

As you might guess, my school days couldn't arrive quickly enough for Mum—she was desperate to get rid of me. Even Heather was looking forward to some well-earned rest. I never wanted to go to school. I hated every school I went to. I would do anything to avoid going. All I wanted to do was to stay home and play.

The two things I hated about school were the discipline and boredom. The discipline I could not tolerate because I thought it was unnecessary. And the boredom of sitting in a classroom attempting to do mathematics, physics, or geography was complete torture. I just had this sneaking suspicion that learning about Newton's theory wasn't actually going to play a huge part in *my* future. The only subjects I enjoyed were soccer, athletics, English, and art. And girls.

The first girlfriend I remember was a girl named Amanda. We were in school together, and I used to follow her around like a puppy dog. Of course, I was only five at the time. My first real kiss came four years later, with a girl who lived at the bottom of my street. Our lawn at that time had three tiers, and if you were on the lowest lawn you couldn't be seen from the house. One day the two of us snuck down there and started kissing. Then there was a girl in school who used to wear very short skirts. Naturally, all the boys used to sit across from her.

By the time I became a teenager, girls were my number-one obsession. In fact, whether it was because of them or because of the general hormonal rushes of adolescence, I was always in a kind of torment. I think it's fair to say that I was the world's worst teenager. From fifteen to seventeen, I was always running away. Like clockwork, every month or so I would fight with my parents—usually my mum—and then pack a bag with a toothbrush and some jeans and a shirt and head out. And not a small bag, for some reason, but a large, unwieldy suitcase. I didn't have a car, so I would just walk out of the house with my huge suitcase, get about fifty yards from the house, realize I had nowhere to go, and then hide with the suitcase for a few hours. Then, after my mood had blown over, I would creep back into the house, scowling at Mum, who of course knew that she had won the battle.

I lost my virginity when I was seventeen to a girl who was attending Windsor Technical College. She was cute—they all were—but we broke up after we went to a party on my motorbike. To be more precise, we broke up during the party, because I saw her making out with one of the teaching assistants. I was heartbroken. The next day, I called her up and uttered what has to be the most pitiful line in the history of romance: "Can I have my crash helmet back?"

Nicholas had been sent away to boarding school, but I was kept at home to attend the local private school. I was thrilled that he had been sent and not me. But after a few months, the headmaster told my mum that they were going to throw me out, so I was packed up and sent to the Dover School to join Nicholas. It was harder for me to leave home at that age—I was fourteen or fifteen at the time—than if I had been younger, because I was old enough to know that this wasn't going to be summer camp. I remember arriving at Dover and heading down to the trunk room to put my trunk away, knowing I wouldn't see it again until I went home for the holidays. That was a miserable sensation.

The first night I was there, I was in a melodramatic mood, and I wrote a letter home that was one for the ages. It went something like this:

> *Dear Mum and Dad, I hope you're happy to finally have got rid of me. I also hope you're happy in your centrally heated warm house and you have a lot to eat. Because I am lying in a dormitory which has icicles on the inside, and there is nothing to eat. I'm freezing cold and hungry. I hope you're finally satisfied —Simon.*

There were six houses, which were basically big buildings where the students slept, and the whole experience was a bit like Harry Potter. It was British boarding school at its worst: The older boys beat up younger boys, and there were more rules than

I knew what to do with. That was also around the time that coeducation was starting to infiltrate the system. We had about three hundred boys, and about six girls, and of course guys at that age would go after anything. Some of these girls weren't exactly beauty queens, but you'd never know it from the attention that they got. I expect they had a rude awakening later on in their lives.

The system was oppressive. I was never caned at school, or beaten by professors, but at one point I was caught drinking with a bunch of friends at a Dover pub. We technically weren't allowed to leave school, but we would sneak out most evenings. Somehow, some creepy teacher's assistant was there and spotted us, and reported us. The teaching assistants were pitiful, absolute sneaks. The next day, I was called in by the housemaster, who told me that he knew I had been there with my friend David, but that they needed the identities of three of the other boys. I refused to give them up. They pressured, and I kept refusing, and in the end I was suspended for five weeks. I was delighted with the five-week holiday, but Mum was very disappointed in me, and she tried to make me do heavy labor at home—chop trees, that kind of thing. When I finally headed back to school, I had only two goals. Number one: Smoke as many cigarettes as possible. Number two: Leave school at the earliest possible age. In England at the time, the earliest possible age was sixteen. That was fine by me; I had absolutely no intention of going into any job where qualifications were necessary. A few of us were even put into a special category because we were so useless. We were given the option of either having tutors to improve our grades or learning to play tennis. To this day, tennis is still my best sport.

Having fluffed my way through every academic challenge, I finally left school at the age of seventeen. My prospects looked bleak, and to make things worse I had no idea what I wanted to do with my life. While Mum and Dad had their own ideas of what I *should* do—like taking an office job or becoming a real estate agent—I had no real idea of what I wanted to do. All I did know was that I wanted to make money. *Real* money. I credit my parents with this: From a very early age, they made us earn our own pocket money. But pocket money wasn't enough. I soon became obsessed with getting rich. From the age of eight I used to make money by cleaning cars on a regular basis. I made quite a lot from this, about £1 a car, and I would do maybe ten cars a day. Later, as I got older, I worked as a babysitter, a window cleaner, a carol singer, and a waiter in Elton John's restaurant in London. I think I lasted two days there before being asked to leave—I was the worst waiter in the world. It was clear that waiting tables wasn't the career for me. But what was?

False Starts

As I considered my future, the one thing I knew for sure was that I couldn't look to my peers for an example. Most of my friends were still in college, or taking a year off to travel the world. For me that was never an option. I had no desire whatsoever to hike across the dusty plains of Australia roughing it as a backpacker. I wanted to earn money, not waste my time.

At this point, my parents were panicking about my future prospects, and they weren't the only ones. Growing up in a celebrity atmosphere had given me a taste for the world of entertainment. But to work in the music industry or films would have been considered just a pipe dream in those days. Particularly as I had no experience or qualifications, apart from an overdeveloped ego. In other words, I was perfectly qualified.

Dad clearly had his own views on what I should do for a living. But they didn't fit with mine. One evening he came looking for me in my bedroom, where I would sneak off to smoke cigarettes and listen to my records. In 1977, punk rock was injecting new energy into the British pop scene, but it left me cold. I was more interested in American pop, in bands like Fleetwood Mac (who had released their immensely popular *Rumours* album) and the Eagles (their song "Hotel California" became my anthem for the summer).

Dad was on a mission that night, and anxious to pin me down about my future, or lack of it. I didn't hear him enter the room with the Eagles' "New Kid in Town" blaring from the speakers. He motioned to me to turn down the music, sat down on one of my large yellow bean bags, and almost toppled backward. I then listened to him (in quiet desperation) as he tried to talk up the same boring career ideas, which involved real estate or retailing. His sermon had the same effect on me as listening to a Perry Como record. Painful.

The following morning, Mum tipped me off that Dad had come up with a cunning plan to kick-start my career by lining me up with a host of job interviews that he had organized through his business colleagues. I'm sure he meant well, somewhere deep down in the recesses of his heart, but to me those interviews seemed—and still seem—like a particularly sadistic torture regimen. I couldn't avoid them forever, as they were suggested by my parents, who loved me (and were now getting desperate), but I did my best to do my worst at each and every job interview that was inflicted upon me.

Career Number One: Simon the Builder

Dad was a qualified surveyor, and he had had this strange notion that I would benefit by following in his muddy footsteps into the building trade. "It's better than doing nothing, son," he used to say. Wrong, I thought.

To keep the peace, I finally agreed to attend a two-day training course to learn about building materials. That was my first big mistake. In the early hours of the morning Dad drove me to Birmingham, which is known in Britain as "The Midlands" because it's in the middle of nowhere. The company's training division was based there—managed by one of Dad's mates, of course. My poor father spent the whole two-hour car journey vainly attempting to sell me on the virtues of a career in the building industry. Cue Perry Como again.

We arrived in Birmingham at 11 A.M. in the pouring rain. I was horrified; the place looked like one gigantic building site. There were trucks and giant diggers everywhere, and the noise was just horrendous. After wading through the mud and rubble for close to an hour, I had seen enough. I turned to Dad and said, "Are you completely mad? I am not staying here a minute longer, let alone two nights. It's dreadful."

He looked shell-shocked for a second. "I take it you are not interested, then," he replied sarcastically.

"No," I said. "Not in a million years."

We drove home in the Jaguar in complete silence while he puffed and chewed angrily on his cigar.

Career Number Two: Simon at the Supermarket

My next stop was an interview with Tesco, one of Britain's largest supermarket chains. Once again Dad had a hand in this debacle; he knew one of the top bosses at Tesco, and he was able to get me into a trainee program where the pay was quite good. Dad's bogus enthusiasm was hardly contagious. He told me that if I started off as a trainee manager and proved my worth, I could go on to become a regional store manager—whoopee! Still, I did need the money—Dad had stopped his weekly handouts to fuel my smoking habit—so I felt resigned to at least take a flier at every single harebrained career idea that he came up with.

I arrived at Tesco's London headquarters and was quickly ushered into the tiniest office I had ever seen. Behind the desk sat a middle-aged man with a droopy mustache wearing a gray suit with leather patches on the elbows. Before I had time to sit down, he was already eyeing me up and down disapprovingly.

Finally he said, "May I ask why you are wearing jeans?"

"Well, I *am* wearing a jacket," I replied.

"But why are you wearing jeans?" he repeated.

I was getting really bored. "I didn't know that a suit was a requirement for the job," I said.

He just glared at me.

"You do not walk into my office for a job wearing jeans. I don't even want to interview you."

Now I'd heard enough. "As a matter of fact, I don't really want to end up as a fifty-year-old bore, sitting in an office the size of a telephone booth, wearing a cheap suit. So I think we are both happy to end this now."

As I got up to walk out, he shouted after me, "You can't talk to me like that, you know."

"I just did," I said, slamming the door behind me.

Career Number Three: Civil Simon

The third time around, my dad went completely over the top. Believe it or not, he thought it would be a great idea for me to apply for a job in the British Civil Service as a trainee law clerk. (Number-one criteria for the job: "Are you the most boring person in the world?") Quite frankly, it was the most bizarre idea I'd ever heard in my life. By this time I was beginning to get the distinct impression that I was going to have a permanent career attending interviews for the dullest jobs in Britain: All very amusing, but it didn't exactly pay well.

The day of my Civil Service interview, I sat in a waiting room for what seemed like hours. At some point during this interminable wait, a middle-aged woman handed me a fact sheet illustrating the earning potential within the Civil Service, should I be lucky enough to get through the interview process. Lucky enough? If I joined at age eighteen, I learned, I could earn as much as £12,000 a year by the time I was age sixty-five. Twelve thousand pounds a year! That was roughly $15,000. There was absolutely no chance that I was going to sit in a stuffy office as a budding law clerk for the next fifty years. Finally, after hours of waiting, I was summoned into a vast room to be faced with a panel consisting of three very stony-faced judges. I think that this is what's known in literature as foreshadowing.

The one female member of the panel, who bore a strong resemblance to Anne Robinson, the host of *The Weakest Link,* proceeded to ask me a whole host of meaningless questions to which I responded with complete indifference. After a few minutes, she rose from her chair and issued her verdict. "Mr. Cowell," she said, "I'm afraid to say that you are the most unsuitable candidate we have ever had the misfortune to interview." This was music to my ears.

Still intent on getting the last word, I turned to face the judges. "Thank you all for saving me from a fate worse than death," I said.

Career Four: Simon on the Big Screen

Some weeks later, having received a rather sulky letter of rejection from the Civil Service, Dad finally conceded defeat in his bid to take my career to new lows. At the same time, he confessed to Mum that he had a sneaking suspicion I had sabotaged every job interview he had sent me to. Smart man.

At that point, I decided that it was time to do something

about my own career. I knew that without any qualifications I would have to take a job at the very bottom of the ladder. I was interested in film, music, and television; I knew that any of these industries would be great fun, and I had a feeling that you could probably make a fortune. I decided to call my cousin, Malcolm Christopher, who worked at Elstree Studios, and ask if he had any jobs available.

It turned out that Malcolm was the production manager on a new television series, and he quickly agreed to take me on for a three-month trial as a runner. Mum was thrilled; Dad just grunted and said it wouldn't last. I was beside myself with joy. I wasn't in the Civil Service, or at a building site. Instead, I was working in the same studio where they had shot *Star Wars*. True, I was making only £15 a week and working from 5 A.M. until 7 P.M. And true, my job wasn't traditionally glamorous. Being a runner meant exactly that—I spent my long days running errands for other people, errands that included buying hemorrhoid treatments for the rather creepy executive producer. Still, I worked like a Trojan. I never stopped running. I was never late and always friendly to everyone on the set. Everyone liked me, apart from the hemorrhoidal executive producer. He was arrogant, vain, and outspoken, and spent most of the day strutting around the studio issuing orders while forgetting to use the word "please." He was also knocking-off his secretary. It sounded like the perfect job.

At the end of my three months, Malcolm went to see the producer, saying, "Look, we want to keep Simon on—it's only

£15 per week and he's worth every penny." Somewhat predictably, he said no; he said that he didn't have money in the budget to employ a runner.

When Malcolm broke the news to me, I was struck dumb. Malcolm was embarrassed for me. "Look, Simon," he said, "I'll pay the £15 a week out of my own pocket. Just carry on working. But keep your head down when the executive producer is around." Grateful as I was to Malcolm, this proved easier said than done. It made me nervous, and I would resort to hiding whenever the executive producer showed up on the set. Inevitably, one day he caught me squatting on my heels under a desk. He pretended he hadn't seen me but told his secretary to get rid of me; he didn't even have the guts to tell me to my face.

Malcolm was really apologetic, but powerless. So in the end I had to walk. My first concern was my parents. The thought of having to tell Dad I had just been sacked filled me with complete horror. I could just see him smiling as he opened up his little book titled *The Most Boring Jobs in the World*. But then I remembered something that my father had always told me: Tenacity is the maker of dreams, and if you want to succeed at something, you have to persevere. It's a trite lesson, maybe, but no less true for its triteness. I went to see another producer friend of Malcolm's, who seemed to like me for all the right reasons. I told him I was desperate to remain at Elstree and find work. He told me that Stanley Kubrick was just about to start going into production on a film called *The Shining*.

With Malcolm's help I immediately applied to work on the

film as a runner. Armed with a dazzling reference from Malcolm, I got the job. As I walked through the studio on my way home that evening, I could see the workers putting the final touches to the set where they had constructed the spooky Overlook Hotel that features throughout *The Shining*. I was in the film business. Two days later, I bumped into the producer as I was walking into the studio gates. "I've got some bad news for you," he said. "Stanley Kubrick won't hire runners." Apparently, I wasn't in the film business after all.

At this point, fate intervened. Though I didn't know it, Mum was convinced that my dream of working in the entertainment industry was a viable one. But not at Elstree. Aware that my contract there was coming to an end, she had sent a letter to EMI Music Publishing asking whether there were any vacancies in the mailroom. EMI was known to us for other reasons, as my father ran their property division, and soon enough a man named Peter Schmidt wrote back to her saying that there was a vacancy available.

A week later, I went in to meet the head of personnel at EMI. He had a star on his door, which kind of put me off a bit, but he was a nice guy and we immediately struck up a rapport. I was given an hour-and-a-half interview—in those days you were interviewed not just for your ability to sort mail, but for your overall career potential. The mailroom was a place from which you could work your way up.

The following day, Peter phoned me. "Simon," he said, "we have decided to offer you a job in the EMI mailroom." I always knew that wearing jeans to an interview would one day pay off.

The very same day I was given the job at EMI, Stanley Kubrick happened to attend a charity dinner, where he was seated at the same table as Dad. Kubrick had already agreed to purchase Abbots Mead from Dad for rather a large sum of money, and as a result Dad and Stanley proceeded to celebrate the deal by consuming vast quantities of bourbon, during which time Dad skillfully persuaded Kubrick to reconsider giving me a job as a runner on *The Shining*. Dad was pretty good—on bourbon. Now I had two job offers on the same day.

By the following morning, I was totally confused. I had been happy working in the film business and learned a lot during my three months at Elstree. And up to that point, I hadn't seriously considered a career in the music industry. Plus, there was the Kubrick problem; Dad felt that we would be letting down the director if we didn't accept his generous offer. So we compromised: I decided to go to Elstree the following morning, and meet up with my potential boss on *The Shining* to see if that would help influence my decision.

The next day, as I entered the studio gates, I noticed a crowd of about thirty men milling about, most of whom were in their forties or fifties. I was curious to know what they were waiting for so early in the morning, and I asked a guy at the end of the line. "What are we queuing for?" he said, gaping at me. "For work, that's what we're queuing for, mate." Suddenly it dawned on me. Jobs here were really scarce, and if you were lucky enough to get one, it wasn't necessarily a job for life. If this was the state of the British film business, I thought, well, then, bring on the music.

As soon as I got home, I phoned EMI and asked when I could start work. Lucky me. Lucky music business.

The mailroom at EMI was a tiny basement office with high ceilings and bars on the windows. Though I was supposed to learn to deliver the mail, from my first day on the job I began planning and scheming my way to the top of the business. I thought it would be easy. It wasn't. In fact, it was downright tedious, but I never gave up. Determination and just a tiny bit of self-belief prevailed. This was *my* first audition, and I desperately wanted to make it through to the next round.

In many ways I was glad that I had started my career on the very bottom rung of the business. It was there that I learned how to deal with people—and not just those who couldn't sing. For me the biggest learning curve was what I learned about human nature. As a mailroom boy, you get to meet people at all levels of the business. It was obvious to me that the people on the bottom rung looked up to those at the top, and the ones at the top invariably looked down on those at the bottom. But my parents taught me that it doesn't matter how powerful or lowly your position is—you should still always treat people around you with manners and respect. Well, most of the time anyway.

On my first day in the job, I was surprised to learn that mailroom employees were not allowed to use the main entrance. Instead, we were told to go through the garages at the rear of the building. There I was greeted by this young guy wearing the

I DON'T MEAN TO BE RUDE, BUT . . .
Punk Music Sucks

At the time I entered the music business, punk music was all
the rage, especially in England. When the whole lot of rubbish
finally crumbled in the late seventies, I breathed a huge sigh of
relief. I hated punk. It was sensationalistic, full of ugly people,
and no fun at all. Most of the band members couldn't sing a
note or even play an instrument. At the height of the punk
movement, there were a lot of people in the music business
who had never been to see a punk band play live. One day a
somewhat overenthusiastic (but pretty) music PR representative
invited me to see one of the overhyped bands who were about
to be signed to a major label. Feeling a touch apprehensive, and
clearly overdressed, I entered a sweaty basement club in London's Soho district. When the band came onstage, they proceeded to jump up and down as if on pogo sticks. The audience
spat beer at them and the band spat back. Great! I came out of
the gig completely covered in spit—not one of my better nights
out—and the band was crap. Punk wasn't anarchy; it was a
sham, and a sham that didn't even sell many records. It was just
a fad. By the time the Sex Pistols attempted to conquer America,
the writing was already on the wall. At a Sex Pistols gig in Texas,
Johnny Rotten walked out onstage wearing a T-shirt that said,
"You cowboys are all a bunch of fucking maggots." The lights
went out and the gig ended in a riot. It was the band's obituary.
Fortunately, America saw them for what they were, dreadful
musicians who couldn't sing.

biggest smile on his face I'd ever seen. "Hi, I'm Colin Smith," he said. "You are my replacement."

I said, "So why are you so happy?"

"You haven't met the two guys you're working for yet," he replied.

I followed Colin into the mailroom. It was the worst room I have ever seen in my life. It was literally dark, damp, and airless.

With his smile broadening, Colin introduced me to Vic and Ron. Ron was adorable; he was about sixty-five and had the shakes but a kindly face. Sadly, he was only second in command. His boss was Vic, who turned out to be a right arsehole. That's all I needed: a good cop and a bad cop.

Vic clearly wasn't happy about being in the mailroom at such an advanced age. He also resented the fact that my dad managed EMI's property division and was on the board. I didn't give a damn—I had to do the job, not my dad. And while Vic thought that I was going to come in and use my dad's influence, the thought had never even crossed my mind. I suppose I was naive; I didn't realize at the time how much certain people would be wary of me for that reason.

You might think delivering mail is easy. It's not, particularly when you are struggling across Charing Cross Road pushing a mail trolley with one of the wheels about to come off. Nobody had told me that EMI had another office three blocks away, or that twice a day I would have to take my life in my hands by crossing four main roads with a load of mail.

As the new kid on the block, I expected a little bit of flack.

But I wasn't prepared for the way that some of the other employees treated me simply because I was a post boy. It was unbelievable; it was as if they considered me the lowest form of life. But never once did I let their snide comments deter me from my main purpose. If anything, it just spurred me on.

For that first year, I was on cloud nine because I had constant access to people who were very influential in the music industry. Even then, I didn't give a hoot what the etiquette was supposed to be. I would just barge into an office and ask for a better job. But after a while, it was apparent I was getting nowhere fast. I was still earning £25 a week and I felt it could take years to get out of the mailroom. Furthermore, my division of EMI was a music publishing company—and I soon learned that the real sexy job in this business was to work for a record label.

One day I found out that there was a job opening at Ariola Records, which was part of BMG. Ariola was what they called an independent and was considered a very cool label. Someone I knew tipped me off that the post boy had just left, and the next day I phoned up and said that I would be very interested in taking the job. I explained that I had always wanted to work for a record label and had put in a year at EMI. I essentially pleaded for an opportunity.

In the end, the man at Ariola said no, that I wasn't qualified enough. I was absolutely shattered. That night I went home and told my parents that I wanted to leave the music industry. What made it even worse was the fact that my younger brother,

Nicholas, had left college and gotten a job as a real estate agent. He was earning £250 a week with a company car. Meanwhile, I was making £25 a week to deliver mail and be ridiculed.

I told Dad I'd had enough. I wasn't getting anywhere. I didn't think they were ever going to promote me. I wanted to leave and do what Nicholas was doing.

I could see Dad struggling to hold back a smirk. "Are you absolutely sure about this?" he said.

"Yes," I said. "I'm positive. I've been there a year and a half now, and it looks like I'm never going to get out of the mailroom."

So out came Dad's book of jobs again—and you guessed it, the book fell open at "P" for Property. He picked up the phone and immediately got me a job at the snottiest firm of real estate agents in the world: Hillier Parker.

Within a week, I had left the music business and was assigned to work for some boring little jerk who was about thirty-five years old. He had thick, ugly glasses and was losing his hair. He didn't like his job very much, and he didn't like me at all. We worked in the commercial division, so most of the job involved tallying sums on calculators, which I kept getting wrong. I opened his post, which I was good at, and made him tea.

After a week I went to Mr. Boring. "Look," I said. "I would actually like to be doing something more than punching numbers into a calculator and making you tea."

"Okay," he said with a nasty little smile on his face, "I've got just the job for you."

"What is it?" I asked.

"Canvassing," he replied.

Canvassing meant that I had to walk the entire length of Oxford Street (three miles), stand outside every shop, write down the name and phone number, and then move on to the next address. When I had finished, I had to cross the road and start doing all the shops down the opposite side of the road. And it was February—the snow was coming down, the wind was howling, and I had no coat. I don't recall how long this exercise took, but it was at least a week. Finally, I got back to the office with the list and handed it to my boss. He looked at it and said, "I can't read your handwriting. Do it all again."

I had never been so depressed in my life. It was the worst job I'd ever had. I had left the mailroom hoping to improve my station; instead, I had sunk lower. Was this my future?

Fortunately, once again fate stepped in. Dad received a phone call from the managing director of EMI Publishing. He hadn't realized that I had left the company, and he told Dad that he wanted me to come back and work in the international division, which represented the writers and catalogues from American companies.

Dad immediately phoned me up at my office with the news. "Will you take the job?" he said.

"Yes," I said. "When can I start?"

There was one last thing I needed to do before I left Hillier Parker. I went straight to my boss's office with a smug look on my face. "So how are my job prospects going?" I asked him.

He looked up from his calculator and said, "I don't really think you have the right attitude to be an estate agent."

"Oh," I said, "is that right? Well, having thought about it, I'm not qualified to be a boring old fart like you, and you're absolutely correct—I don't have the right attitude. So you can stick your job up your arse. I'm leaving today. Good-bye."

That evening when I got home, I was on a high as I prepared myself for my reentry into the music business. This time I was determined not to screw things up.

My high lasted until nine the following morning, when I walked into my new office at EMI. The job wasn't quite what I had expected. There were only about ten people working in the department, and we were supposed to take songs and go around to record labels and see if we could get well-known artists to record the songs we represented.

Not yet an expert in office politics, I was unaware that there was a secretary in another division whose boss fancied her and had promised her *my* job. This led to the rumor that I got the job only because my dad was a pal of the managing director. Never mind that I had worked in the mailroom for nearly two years. Nobody in the department would talk to me or even look at me. Welcome back, Simon.

On the
Right Track

Despite the ice-cool reception I received when I first
arrived at my new job at EMI, I kept my head down and struggled on. Uncomfortable as it was being ostracized by most of the
staff, office politics bored me. I saw these idiots as a colossal
waste of time and wasn't about to let them get the best of me. I
was in, I was there, and I was going to make it.

At first, I gathered the whole catalogue, found a room with a
tape player, and began to go through every single song. There
were thousands of them. Some were country, some pop; some
had been recorded by American artists but not covered by anyone in the U.K. I noted the specific details of every song and
then drew up a "hit list" of U.K. artists that I thought would

work well with them. After six months, I had gained a better knowledge of the company's international song catalogue than anyone else in my department. As my confidence grew, I was ready to take my next step, which was to contact all the major record labels and start trying to sell our songs to their artists. The only obstacle I had to overcome was the A&R men.

Without question, A&R people were then the biggest arseholes in the music business. A&R stands for Artists and Repertoire. These are the guys who are responsible for signing artists, choosing the material for the artist, getting the right producer, and generally keeping up with music trends—well, that was the theory anyway. I soon discovered why I hated A&R people. My very first meeting was with a guy called Paul, who was head of A&R at one of the major labels. Paul was well known in the business as being a little unhinged. I soon learned why. As I sat down opposite him in his office, he slowly began to take off his shoes and socks and then put his bare feet on the desk in front of my face as I talked. It was an act of intimidation, pure and simple. Nowadays I would probably just laugh at him, but that day, on my first pitch, I wasn't amused. As my pitch came to a close, Paul just looked at me blankly. "I don't think there's any decent material there for me," he said. "Come back when you have something hot." I left feeling frustrated. I knew I had good material—he was just an idiot who didn't know what he was doing. The funny thing was, about a month later I had gotten about fifteen or twenty songs placed with major artists on other labels and then he called me for an appointment. I told him to stuff it.

Despite the minor setbacks caused by crazed A&R men, I remained committed to learning my trade. But increasingly I was finding myself bored working at EMI. I was very ambitious and already had my own ideas. I was also beginning to realize that this was a business you had to teach yourself—and that if I was going to do well, I would have to take risks.

So a year after I joined EMI I decided to quit my job and make a rather disastrous attempt to start my own music publishing company. This ill-fated mission lasted about as long as an interview for one of Dad's bizarre jobs, but this time I learned a harsh lesson. Ellis Rich was my immediate boss at EMI. He had worked there for eighteen years and was looking for a change. We had begun to get on well, and this led him to suggest that we start our own publishing company. Naively I asked, "What does that entail?"

"Making a lot of money," he said. "I think we can get funding, we can own the company, and it can be our business." I was still very young, and I didn't really have much experience, but I knew that Ellis did, and that made me feel more comfortable about the idea. He offered me a joint partnership. Deep down, I worried that we might be getting in over our heads. But I was tempted and flattered by Ellis's offer and his confidence in me. In the end, I chose to leave and started E&S Music.

Within a day of moving into our new offices in Soho, London, I realized I had made a big mistake. We didn't have the funding to do it properly: We couldn't get the business off the ground, and many of the fundamentals of running an independent company were foreign to us. After a week or so, I went back to see Ron White, who was the managing director at EMI. After overdoing the small talk, I finally summoned the courage to say, "Look, Ron, I think I have made a big mistake. I admit I was wrong. Can I have my old job back?"

Ron just stared blankly at me. "No you can't," he said. "I trusted you, Simon, and I was going to nurture you. I was going to groom you for the top, but you've betrayed my trust. I can't have you back here." I left the room feeling reprimanded, like I was back at school. Now I had no choice but to try and make it work with Ellis.

E&S Music was set up as an independent publishing company. We had signed a few writers, but the only way we were going to be able to survive was by getting representation in each country—and, more important, for each country to advance us money based on future earnings. Without these advances we were never going to survive the year. Our best shot was to go to America and try to drum up some business. It was my first trip to Los Angeles, and the place seemed like paradise to me. On top of that, the prospects seemed good, at least at first—we had six or seven really positive meetings with publishing companies. Everyone, it seemed, wanted to work with us. On the way back on the plane, Ellis and I were both on a high and thought we had cracked America. But the joke was on us. We never heard from anyone we met in L.A. again. That's the thing about Los Angeles: It's a very difficult place to try and make it from the bottom up. It only works if you're dealing from a position of strength—a theory that I would test a little later.

About a year later, I decided I had to cut my losses. The business wasn't making money, and we were still struggling to get further financing. I was unhappy and wanted out, so I told Ellis I was quitting. He wasn't pleased, but he understood that I was ambitious and wanted to get out of music publishing. It was a bad period for me, but an experience that helped me focus on where I thought my future in the music business really was. Ellis went on to run his own successful publishing company.

What I wanted to do was to make records. Hit records, preferably. But with my history in the business, it was unlikely that any record label would hire me as a producer or an A&R guy. What I did feel was that I had an instinctive understanding of what it took to generate a hit. I understood publishing, A&R, and a bit about how to market records—but what my time at EMI had shown me above all was that you first had to have great songs. And if they were great songs, they would sell forever. I wanted to prove to myself that my instinct for finding hits was actually correct. That's when I met up with an astute manager named Iain Burton.

Iain was about six years older than me. A former dancer, he had already made a lot of money from his management company supplying dancers for pop videos and TV. I had seen Iain a few times while I was at EMI, when he came in with artists he represented, and I had met him socially. That's how I heard he was looking to start a record label. While he had little knowledge of running a label, he was prepared to be an entrepreneur and take a risk. And let's face it: He was taking a huge gamble starting a record label with me. But like me, Iain was driven by a true love of music and the will to succeed, and I think that's why we hit it off. He recognized that I had something to prove. We decided to give it a go.

Being able to run things my way for the first time in the record business was a giant step. But I wasn't daunted—I felt I was ready. Iain and I quickly struck a deal, and he agreed to pay me £65 a week. (One lesson I have learned over the years is to never overnegotiate your initial salaries. If things work out afterward, the money will follow. Ask for too much at the beginning and you may not get the job.) One of the upsides to this new job was working out of Iain's offices on South Molton Street. In those days South Molton Street was like a catwalk. The street was lined with trendy clothes shops and cafés, and had quickly become home to London's top model agents. It was an incredible place to be.

At the beginning, we didn't even focus on music. Iain had watched Jane Fonda make a fortune from launching the first ever exercise video, and the global success of that endeavor had given birth to a lucrative market in aerobics videos. Everyone in Britain wanted to jump on the bandwagon, but Iain got there first and made a video with a British choreographer named Arlene Philips. Arlene was a friend and client of Iain's and one of the most successful choreographers in Britain. Just about every major recording artist in the world wanted her to work on their videos, and she already had a profile from working on TV with a very successful dance act called Hot Gossip. The video sold hundreds of thousands of copies, and our new label, Fanfare Records, was born.

I was now running my own record label. This was a godsend, and it was also a problem. I didn't have a secretary, didn't have a mailroom boy, and didn't have any A&R men. Oh—and I didn't have any recording artists, either.

This was all to change when I met a black singer from Seattle named Sinitta. It was to be my first big break.

We met in a nightclub, and I fancied her like mad. Sinitta was eighteen years old, tiny, with long dark hair that went almost to her waist. I gave her some cheesy line about running a record label, and she said, "That's cool—I'm a singer. Why don't you make a record with me? Let's meet up and talk about it." Of course, I didn't want to meet up to talk business. I wanted to take her out.

The following day, she turned up at my office and played me some demo tapes she had made. I was shocked to discover that she had a great pop voice. And as I already knew from the nightclub, she could dance. (Her mother, I would find out later, was Miquel Brown, who had a number of hits in the early seventies, including "So Many Men, So Little Time.") I agreed to sign her up as an artist. It was the least I could do. Sinitta became my first signing, but at the time I had absolutely no idea what I was going to do with her.

This was a rich period of learning for me; in the span of twelve months I would have to learn to single-handedly master everything: signing artists, making records, commissioning videos, and selling records to the retailers, not to mention the mind-numbingly dull issues like managing stock control. With the success of the exercise video Iain had made a lot of money and he was now willing to let me have free rein. What I wanted to do was build a successful record label, and I was determined to succeed at all costs.

I immediately approached a well-known songwriter and asked him to try and come up with some suitable tracks. Two days later, he came back with a song called "So Macho." It was perfect for Sinitta, and the moment I heard it I knew it was going to be a huge hit. I drove straight over to Sinitta's apartment to play it to her. She loved it, and we were both really excited. But while I was there, Iain Burton telephoned me. "Simon," he said, "I need to tell you something." I could tell by his voice he wasn't planning to raise my salary, and there was an uncomfortable pause. "Look," he said, "I have to close down the record label." I was stunned and demanded to know why. "I'm putting all my money into a new project, so I need to close down the label," he said. "So I'm sorry—it's over." We hadn't even started!

Now my mind was racing. "Wait," I said. "Iain, listen. I think we've got a hit record here with Sinitta, and I'm begging you, please don't close this label down. Just give me some money and I'll make this record a hit." I eventually convinced him to give me £5,000 to cover everything, including the video. I had a feeling the video wasn't going to be "Thriller."

The pressure turned out to be a blessing in disguise. The stakes were high, and I was forced to work with a tiny budget and rely on sheer drive and enthusiasm to try to create a hit. I had no idea if it would work, but I knew that if I blew it, I wouldn't even be a one-hit wonder. I made a video for £2,000—and trust me, it looked like it. Then I hired a record plugger, but I told him I would pay him only if he got results. I was desperate. When we finally put the record out, it entered the U.K. charts at around number forty and then stalled. But there was actually some momentum on the sales front—the sales just kept chugging along. So I released it a second time—and nothing. The third time was the charm. Within a few months we had sold just under 900,000 copies and "So Macho" had reached number two on the U.K. pop charts. In the end, we had done the whole thing for just £5,000 and made close to £1 million profit. More important, I had my first hit single. But most important, Iain decided that he wanted to reinvest in the record label. What a surprise!

With my job and the future of the label now secure, I pondered what to do next. I honestly believed that Sinitta had tremendous potential beyond this first hit. By this time she had a loyal fan base and had built up a huge following. It was just a question of finding the right song for a follow-up single.

It was at this critical stage in my career that I began to understand the true value of using the best producers and writers. I went on to learn that without a consistent hit writing and production team behind you, it is almost impossible to launch a pop star who doesn't write his or her own material. There was a buzz at the time about three new record producer/writers called Stock, Aitken & Waterman. Pete Waterman was the guy who had put the three of them together. A former gravedigger, he had been a successful club DJ before becoming one of Britain's most successful record producers and songwriters. He would go on to have more than thirty number-one hits and seventy top-twenty records during the 1980s and '90s. Pete has claimed that he has sold an astonishing 500 million singles in his career. Years later he would sit alongside me as a judge on *Pop Idol,* the U.K. version of *American Idol.* Today he is one of my best friends in the music industry.

Back then, however, Pete was just starting out. His first real hit was by a singer named Hazel Dean. The record went to number three, and when I heard it I knew instantly that whoever had written and produced it were geniuses.

I was desperate to get Stock, Aitken & Waterman to write a song for Sinitta—I knew I had one shot to take her to the next level, and I couldn't afford anything less than a worldwide smash. Since I have never been shy about opening my mouth, I phoned up Pete Waterman and said, "We haven't spoken before. My name's Simon Cowell. I look after a singer named Sinitta, and I would like to come and talk to you about working with us." He agreed to meet with me.

I arrived at his studio, which in those days consisted of crumbling plaster walls and discarded plastic coffee cups all over the floor. Abbey Road it wasn't. We had to sit on wooden crates. At the time, Pete was in his mid-forties, with thinning gray hair.

He was really full of himself. It was a bit like looking in the mirror—apart from the hair.

"I have a hunch that you guys are going to be huge," I began.

"So do I," he said.

"Well, I want to hire you to produce a follow-up for Sinitta."

Pete smiled and said, "I'm too busy."

"On what?" I asked him, looking around at this dump of a recording studio.

Pete just winked and said, "You'll see."

I didn't really know why, but I was convinced that Pete was the man who could provide the next hit for Sinitta, and more. I didn't want to let the moment pass, so I tried another angle. "If I find the right song, will you produce it for us?" I asked him.

Pete began to laugh. "You don't take no for an answer, do you?"

At that point he more or less threw me out of the studio, saying that if I sent him some songs he would give me his opinion, that's all—if he had the time.

Weeks later, Pete's career exploded. Stock, Aitken & Waterman owned pop music and had the music industry eating out of its hand. With hits for artists including Donna Summer, Dead or Alive, Bananarama, Kylie Minogue, and Rick Astley, Stock, Aitken & Waterman became the most successful writing and production team in history. There was just one problem—where was my Sinitta hit?

I was sharp enough to know that Pete could become my mentor. He had knowledge of the industry and a cultural savvy that I craved, and I wanted to learn what it took to get to his level. Every day that I could get away from the office, I showed up at Pete's studio and followed his every move. I was still looking for that elusive song for Sinitta, and I knew that he was the one to help. He was arrogant, conceited, and rude—and a genius. My kind of guy.

In those days, Pete's studio was total chaos. People were constantly coming and going, and artists were in the studio recording night and day. No one thought it odd that I would drift in from time to time. But after a few months of being there, Pete pulled me to one side. "Simon," he said, "am I mistaken in thinking that you've turned up most days for the past few months? What exactly are you doing here?"

"Seeing how you work," I said. "Learning the business."

"Well, I'm not going to pay you," he warned.

"I don't want you to pay me," I said.

Now he was getting irritated. "Then what the fuck do you want?"

"Just to follow you around," I said. And that's what I did. When I had the opportunity, I would go into the studio and watch the way Pete handled the engineers and producers during a recording. I began to learn all about what it takes to produce a hit. A song can be mind-blowing, but it's the production and the final mix that determine how successful the record will be.

Years later, Pete would tell me about the first time he saw me in the studio with the boy band Westlife, my first bona fide breakout success. He noticed the way I expressed myself to the engineers, how I told them what I wanted from the final mix, and he said it was precisely the same way that he worked in the studio. When I first began shadowing Pete, I already knew what I wanted to hear, but I had to learn how to tell the engineers and producers what I wanted. That, in essence, is what I learned from Pete Waterman: the language and the know-how. It was also Pete who told me that there is only one key area of pop music: the song.

Ironically, after all that education, I was still looking for that elusive second song for Sinitta, and I still believed Pete was the person to help. In the meantime, Sinitta had been making a good living touring the clubs and doing public appearances around the country. But at this point she was still my only artist. I had a responsibility to make her successful. If I could take her to the next level, the Fanfare label would also start to have credibility. So I continued to make a nuisance of myself and badger Pete to write a song at every opportunity. Whenever I did, he would just frown and say, "I'm too busy to write songs. You find me the right track and I'll produce it for you." Each time I thought I had found a hit song, I would play it and he would shout over it, "Crap, crap, crap . . . you don't know what you're talking about. Come back to me when you've got something worth listening to." His ranting only made me more determined to succeed. (I'm often asked if I can take criticism, and I always think back to these days, when the tough feedback of someone who knew more than I did helped me so much more than fake praise.)

One day I read an article in the newspaper about the new trend of celebrities stepping out with younger guys. Toyboys,

I DON'T MEAN TO BE RUDE, BUT . . .
Michael Jackson Is a Spoiled Brat

Without a doubt, Michael Jackson made some of the best pop records of all time. If you were to list the fifty best pop songs in history, you would have many Michael Jackson songs on that list: "Billie Jean," "Thriller," "Black or White." He was a genius. But the last record he released, *Invincible,* was one of the weakest efforts I had ever heard. He went on television and blamed Sony for everything. He said that they weren't behind him, that they were racist; he launched a bitter attack against Tommy Mottola. The simple truth, as anyone who heard the record knows, is that the new record was crap. The songs were weak: He'd lost his spark, his individuality, his edge. The notion that the record company somehow sabotaged him is just idiotic: I'm sure people actually lost their jobs when the record performed badly. The weirdness in his life hasn't helped matters, of course, because it has made it so that he can't be taken seriously. I felt quite bad for him after that documentary with Martin Bashir, because I think it did proceed from bad faith. But he's the equivalent of a Victorian freak show. I'd watch anything on him; it's a train wreck. But it doesn't help him return to being a serious pop artist. If I were entrusted with fixing his career, I would probably tell him to camp outside Quincy Jones's house. Their partnership worked for him. I don't know why he abandoned it. The other producers just failed to understand that you can't make him sound like everybody else. He's *not* everybody else. He's Michael Jackson.

they were called. So I telephoned Pete and said, "I have a great title for a song, 'Toyboy.' I'm sure it will work, Pete, just write the song." He said grudgingly, "Yeah, you're right. It is a good title. I could write a song in about five minutes."

"Okay, do it," I challenged him.

"No!" he shouted. "I'm too bloody busy." He slammed down the phone. I could feel Sinitta breathing down my neck.

Three months later Pete called me, sounding really excited. "Simon, get down to the studio now. I've got your hit!"

"What hit?" I asked.

"'Toyboy,' mate. I've written it."

I will never forget that moment. Even then, I knew it was going to change my life. I raced down to Pete's studio. I could barely breathe. And the second he put it on, I knew it was going to be a smash hit. We brought Sinitta straight into the studio that day and started recording. With Pete's help, "Toyboy" went on to be an even bigger hit for Sinitta than "So Macho." It sold millions of copies all over the world, and it finally helped to get my label taken seriously. But there was still a long way to go.

Hitting the
Big Time

Fanfare Records and Sinitta continued to have a string of hits throughout the 1980s. We began to break her as an artist in other parts of the world, most notably Japan, and in Britain she became one of the biggest-selling pop artists; her earning potential was now phenomenal. The downside was that our relationship deteriorated. It was impossible to date her and be her record label, and we eventually agreed it would be just business from now on.

By this time, I had accomplished two things: I had broken an artist worldwide and I had now become good friends with one of the most successful producers in the business. And more important, I had learned things from Pete that I would never have learned at a major label. The day I met Pete Waterman was easily the most important day of my career.

In the British music business there has always been great importance placed on the idea of integrity and credibility. Punk was seen as having "street cred," which meant that the artists weren't artificially constructed by a record company but represented something real from the clubs and the neighborhoods that would be recognized as legitimate by record buyers. I still think punk was a low point. The first wave of New Romantics—bands like ABC, Duran Duran, and so forth, which picked up on the fashion and style of seventies bands like Roxy Music and David Bowie—fell into the same category, before other artists jumped onto the bandwagon. In the mid-eighties, the ultimate in "non-cred" was to be associated with the country's biggest hitmakers, Stock, Aitken & Waterman. Their songs were simply too commercial for some tastes. Not for me. If I want art, I'll buy it. For me the decision was clear-cut—"street cred" or hit singles. Pop was what I liked and understood. Pop for me would always be the future.

By 1985 my partner, Iain, was looking to expand his business. He had identified a gap in the electronics market, of all things, and developed a number of handheld gadgets, including a currency calculator, which he marketed throughout Europe. For Iain our future lay in diversification; I, however, wanted to keep developing a successful record label. The music industry press at the time saw the growth of independent labels like Fanfare as a healthy alternative to the major labels. I got the feeling Iain didn't agree.

The major difficulty in being a small label is ensuring proper distribution for your records. As a result, Fanfare had struck up a distribution deal with one of the major record labels, BMG. As Iain continued to invest his energies in Fanfare Electronics, I felt he wasn't as committed to investing in the record label with the same verve. Obviously, a lot of the revenue from our chart success had gone to fund Iain's foray into the electronics business, which was frustrating. Soon I learned that certain people at BMG had been charting my course and were looking to hire me to come and work there, and in 1989 I was offered the chance to join BMG Records as an A&R consultant. This was my biggest career break so far. The consultancy meant I would remain independent, and the company promised me free rein on whatever I wanted to do, with one proviso: I had to sell a minimum number of records in the first year if I wanted my option taken up.

Being an A&R consultant meant I had to identify new talent, find new songs, and break as many records as possible. Given the financial security and marketing budget that came with a major label like BMG, it wasn't a hard decision to make. I left Fanfare Records—and, I should say, Iain and I did not part company amicably. I was, however, grateful for the help that he had given me. Iain was the best salesman I have ever met and everything he did reaffirmed my belief that you should never take "No" for an answer.

From the outset I had talks with my bosses at BMG during which I set out my vision. My vision, in short, was television. In 1981, MTV had changed the face of the music industry entirely, and very quickly video became king. In those days, without a really hot video, it was virtually impossible to break a new artist and have a hit record. In the early days of MTV, music videos had small budgets and production values to match—take my Sinitta video as an example—but kids were hooked, and then more imaginative, elaborate, and expensive videos like Peter Gabriel's "Sledgehammer" upped the ante. Very soon record companies were spending more and more money to make their videos slicker and more stylish. The competition for chart position depended on these television spots. Michael Jackson topped everyone by spending $4 million on his "Thriller" video, which helped make the album of the same name the greatest seller of all time. I still think "Thriller" remains the best pop video ever made. Jackson treated the whole thing as you would a movie. He hired John Landis to direct it, after seeing his hit film *An American Werewolf in London.* He even made sure he got the same makeup artists and special-effects specialists to work on the video. He got it just right.

MTV was already a media force, so I wasn't the only one to have the bright idea. But I was the one to have the brightest version of it. For me, it wasn't just about videos but the entire medium of television. I felt that major record companies had failed to understand the importance of TV as a medium for breaking artists. Trying to get radio play with a new artist has always been a nightmare. Television, on the other hand, has a huge captive audience and also the ability to create something unique for an artist—an image and emotion: two very important factors in selling pop music. BMG listened and agreed to let me focus on the small screen.

Around that time, I cut a deal that would change my life. I read in a newspaper that the World Wrestling Federation (WWF) had come over to tour Britain and had sold out Wembley Stadium in twenty-seven minutes. I knew that there were few music artists who could sell out an eighty-thousand-seat venue in that amount of time. So I phoned up the boss at WWF, Vince McMahon, and said, "Have you ever thought about making an album with your wrestlers?"

As luck would have it, one of McMahon's managers was in town the next day and we had a breakfast meeting. I persuaded him that the deal was a good idea, and at my insistence Pete Waterman wrote and produced the album. This would be the first record I released to test this theory of mine. Could I sell an album without any radio play at all and rely solely on the word-of-mouth buzz created by television? The single went to number 3 on the charts and the album went on to sell more than 1.5 million copies throughout Europe. Even though I knew at the time that The Undertaker and Randy Savage certainly weren't what you'd call career artists, the experience proved that I was correct in my thinking. This, I realized, was an area within the industry that I could capitalize on, and possibly even own.

To say that I faced resistance from within the music business was an understatement. At that point, I was at Arista Records, which was one of the labels under the BMG umbrella, and people weren't necessarily thrilled with the idea of signing up television characters. Before the WWF record came out, in fact, one senior executive at the label actually got down on her knees and begged me not to do the deal with the wrestlers. She never believed it would work. Other people at the label wanted credibility. I wanted hits, and I couldn't have cared less about credibility. Still, the constant negativity got to me. I went through a stage when I had records that were succeeding but never quite made it to number one, and I began to have grave doubts about my course. When you're in an environment like that, you need supportive people around you, and I didn't have many.

Still, I knew in my heart that I was right. In fact, after the WWF record came out, I went through a phase where I was somewhat fanatical about making records with television characters and personalities. I set my sights on Zig and Zag, who were puppets on a British television show called *The Big Breakfast*. They were absolutely massive at the time, and everyone in Britain was talking about them. I also signed the Power Rangers, who were the biggest toy phenomenon in history. Those were the days when singles could sell two million copies, and I was very enthusiastic about these two acts. I remember sitting down with my assistant at the time and telling her that if those two records didn't take off, I was going to leave the business for a year. If my instincts about them were wrong, then my entire perspective on the industry was off, and something would have to change.

That was the consensus, certainly. I remember a board meeting in which my assistant and I presented our latest signings to the record label heads. We went through an endless series of flip charts, talked about domestic signings and other boring matters.

Then I raised my hand and announced that I had two major signings: Zig and Zag and the Power Rangers. There were sneers and muffled laughter around the room. A woman named Diana, who was one of the managing directors—the top executive at the label, basically—asked me if she could hear the records before we went any further. "With respect," I said, "if you've got a record by Zig and Zag or the Power Rangers, you can make a calculated guess that they're going to sell a lot of copies."

"Well, I refuse to do anything until I hear the records," she said.

I went to my office and brought back the rough demo I had done with Zig and Zag—it was just a drum track with their sample vocals over the top. I put it on in the meeting, and after fifteen seconds Diana turned off the machine and drew a zero on the flip chart. She didn't think the record had a chance. At that point I got up, shook hands with everybody around the table, and made an announcement. "Just to let you know," I said, "this will be the last time you ever see me again, because I'm walking out of here."

I went straight to the office of John Preston, the chairman of BMG, and told him that he needed to move me to another label or lose me entirely. He called up RCA, another label in the BMG family, and just like that I was transferred. Jeremy Marsh was the managing director and the complete opposite of Diana. He was great fun and very supportive, and to this day remains one of my best friends. Monday morning, at RCA, I brought up the Power Rangers, and they were instantly enthusiastic. I flew to L.A., came back with the deal, and we put both singles out.

Of all the records I have ever put out in my life, these were the most pivotal. If the records hadn't worked it would have proved to me—and the rest of the industry—that I had lost my touch.

By this time, I had begun to think very differently from most people in the music business. Most of my colleagues were obsessed with signing the next coolest rock or alternative band, and I was considered by many to be a laughingstock—a freak. "You're signing wrestlers, puppets, the fucking Power Rangers!" one senior executive screamed at me once. "What kind of future do you have?" Well, that was the point—I felt that I was latching on to something unique that could potentially grow into a fantastic business. I always used to say to people during this period, "Laugh all you want. This is my target practice." In other words, I was still learning. I was beginning to understand trends in the marketplace. And I knew even then that the link between television and music would be even more important in years to come.

Fortunately, I hadn't lost my touch at all. Both the Zig and Zag and Power Rangers tracks were Top 3 singles, and between the two of them RCA sold one and a half million copies. We then sold over a million Power Rangers albums off the back of that one single. It was a huge victory for me, especially given the reluctance of those imbeciles at Arista, most of whom are now out of the business. Would these records touch people the way John Lennon's "Imagine" had? No. But they still found an enormous audience. And they restored my confidence. The fact that I now had somebody who believed in me and the fact that

I had been right meant everything to me. Everyone needs that kind of confidence restorer at some point in their career.

Not every television property was a sure thing. Through the music community, I heard that the comedian Eddie Murphy, who had risen to success in *Saturday Night Live,* was looking to make an album—and not a comedy album, either, but a pop music album. After making contact through his managers, I flew to the United States to have a meeting with him at his house outside New York. Thinking that he was going to play me some tracks on his personal stereo, I was a little surprised to be taken down to the basement, where he had his own state-of-the-art recording studio. An entourage, fifteen strong, surrounded Eddie. It was quite obvious to me that every one of those guys was making a good living off of the Eddie Murphy Music Project. And it was also obvious why: When it came to music, Eddie had a sense-of-humor bypass. He took his new music career seriously—very, very seriously. His music *was* funny, but not in a good way. I asked to hear some of the songs he was thinking of recording, which of course he had written himself. After song twelve, I was losing the will to live. I had run out of fake compliments. Every recording was complete and utter rubbish. Throughout this ghastly session, his entire team of yes-men were busy nodding their heads and smiling like a gospel choir. I turned to Eddie and whispered in his ear, "Is it at all possible that we could have a word in private?" He could see by my face that I was serious, and he told the "choir" to leave the studio. I then explained in no uncertain terms that the songs were not up to standard.

"What's wrong with them?" he asked.

"Eddie," I replied, "they're crap. If you really want to break into pop music, then I suggest you come to the U.K. and work with some of our producers." I actually believed that we could make it work; Bruce Willis had recently released an album that had sold nearly a million copies in Britain.

A week later, I got a call from his manager giving me the details of his traveling party. It read like a scene from *Coming to America*. The entourage included about thirty hangers-on. I calculated that it would cost me close to $500,000 to fly him in to record three or four songs. That was unacceptable. I was on the phone to Eddie straightaway.

"Why do you need all these people?" I asked him.

"Well, that's how we normally travel," he said.

"Okay," I said, "the deal's off." I never spoke to him again. I did hear that he went on to enjoy some success in films.

Another television star that I worked with during my early days at BMG Records was David Hasselhoff. At that time, David was not just a television personality. He had been very successful in Germany, selling millions of records, and he was desperate to break into the U.K. market. I got a call from one of the top executives at BMG in New York who explained that David was one of our biggest-selling artists, and that he really wanted a hit in the U.K. I was basically told, "Get him a hit." While David's image in England was certainly that of a big star, mainly due to the success of *Baywatch,* I had severe doubts that anyone would take him seriously as a singer.

I arranged for a very credible journalist to meet with David in London, and we agreed that the interview would focus on his singing career, and the success he had had in Germany. We met David at his hotel, where he was staying with his sidekick, a guy named Buddy. We sat down at the table, and almost immediately David began to tell a story about how he had just returned from a trip to Africa. "I had this amazing experience while I was there," he said. "I held up my son to the dawn. I can honestly say I have truly discovered the importance of life." Everyone around the table remained silent. It was excruciating. Then, to my horror, David started to cry. The journalist couldn't believe her luck, especially when Buddy pulled out his handkerchief and wiped away the tears as if it were the most natural thing in the world. I had to use every inch of my considerable charm to persuade the reporter not to print the story. Not the best of starts—but the worst was to follow.

I approached Pete Waterman to see if he would work with David and produce some songs. Initially, he said yes, he would be delighted. But several weeks later, after a number of meetings with David, Pete suddenly called, saying he couldn't work with him anymore. "He's just too demanding," he said. "It's too much work."

I was horrified. "Pete," I pleaded, "will you reconsider? He's really excited about working with you."

"Too bad, mate," Pete said. "I'm not doing it."

Two hours later, I got a call from David. "When do we start recording?" he asked.

"Well, actually we're not," I said. "Pete doesn't feel that he can work with you."

"What do you mean he can't work with me?" David demanded. "Doesn't he like my singing?"

"He didn't mention your singing," I told him.

"Right," he said. "Meet me in one hour at the hotel; I'll be in the restaurant." And he slammed down the phone.

When I arrived at the hotel, there were six people sitting with him around a table. As I walked toward them, expecting a big shouting match, I saw that David had a horrible grin on his face. He pulled out a boom box. "So I'm not good enough to work with Pete Waterman, am I?" he said, leering at me. Then he pressed Play; on came the backing track to Jackie Wilson's "Your Love Is Lifting Me Higher," which he proceeded to sing in my face in front of the whole restaurant. Halfway through the song the hotel manager appeared. "If you want to sing in your suite, Mr. Hasselhoff, I can arrange it—but we don't allow it in the dining room." I gave that guy the biggest tip of his career.

In the end we hired a new production and writing team, put David in the studio, and finally gave him a hit record in the U.K. Unfortunately, success didn't improve his dress sense. It fell to me to persuade him not to wear an electric-blue suit while appearing on the iconic British TV show *Top of the Pops*. Street cred? I don't think so.

At my final meeting with him, I couldn't resist having the last word. He was in his hotel suite surrounded by his team of hangers-on. "David," I said, "the problem with you is that you are incredibly precious."

A horrible silence followed, and his entourage looked on in total disbelief. David looked at me and whispered, "Did you just call me precious, Simon?"

I nodded grimly.

"You're absolutely right, Simon!" he shouted. "I am precious." He seemed pleased about this. I always thought David was hysterically funny, though I can't say that his comedy was always intentional. Working with people like him—or Eddie Murphy, for that matter—was quite an education. I grew accustomed to dealing with people who were certain that they had futures as pop stars, even if every single available shred of evidence suggested the exact opposite.

If those two television stars didn't exactly revolutionize pop music, there were two others who did: Robson and Jerome. After the WWF, after Zig and Zag, and after the Power Rangers, I was doing well financially, but not as well as others in the business. I was making a small fortune, but not a large one. And I was, as always, very competitive. I wanted to be the top dog within RCA, and I wasn't happy that other A&R men were having bigger hits than I was. In fact, it made me very depressed. I could talk about teamwork, and the good of the company, and all the other clichés, but why bother? The idea of rooting for your fellow A&R men has always seemed like a big lie to me. I'm as competitive with somebody who works for my company as I am with somebody who works for another label, and in a way it makes it worse. In fact, if a fellow A&R man was happy for my success, I would find that very odd.

Then I had a really lucky break. There was a girl working for our sales division at the time, a very bright girl named Denise Beighton, and she had an uncanny ability to spot a hit record. She just knew. One morning, she walked into my office and said something strange. "By the way, we're getting a ton of phone calls from every retailer in England asking if we're responsible for anything by Robson and Jerome."

"Who are Robson and Jerome?" I said.

Denise laughed. "They're actors in the TV series *Soldier Soldier,*" she said. "Last night they sang a version of 'Unchained Melody,' and the reaction has been amazing." I called the television producer; she said that their office had also been besieged by calls. And then I called up about ten record stores across England—they, too, were getting hundreds of inquiries. I called the producer right back and asked for an introduction to Robson and Jerome, only to be told that they weren't interested. I called their agents and reached the same dead end. It was very frustrating, but I kept on. I needed to talk to them and try to persuade them to release the single. A few weeks later, just before I was going to go on vacation, I received a phone call from someone representing Robson Green. He told me that Robson was going to take legal action if I continued to harass him; at this point, I was sending letters, faxes, hand-delivered notes, everything. No response. I went on vacation, but after a few days I couldn't stand it any longer and flew back to the U.K. When I got back, I kept calling, once a day, twice a day, ten times a day. I just went mental. I wouldn't give up. Eventually, the phone rang and it was Robson Green. "Why are you harassing me and my family?" he screamed.

"Why won't you talk to me?" I said.

"Because I'm not interested," he said. "I don't want to appear on *Top of the Pops*."

That's when I made my offer. "Listen," I said. "Just for one second. If you go in and cut this record for me, I'll give you and Jerome fifty thousand pounds each. Even if we don't put the record out, I'll pay you. Think about it: two hours' work, fifty thousand pounds at worst. And if you like it and you're willing to talk, then we'll talk about a deal."

"Are you prepared to put that in writing?" he said. I couldn't have agreed fast enough. I went to his agent's office immediately.

On the way over, I realized that I had no idea what he looked like. I hadn't seen the show even once. I walked into the office and blurted out, "Simon here." Thankfully, Robson waved back. He was insistent on talking about his television character. For a half hour, I lied through my teeth about my admiration for the show, how important and worthwhile it was. Finally, he asked if I was serious about the deal. I said I was, and I gave him an offer there and then.

I set up the recording date with Pete Waterman's production partners, Mike Stock and Matt Aitken, and they started cutting the record. When I went down to the studio for a check-in, I knew that I had hooked them. Robson and Jerome were sitting in the recording booth listening to the record, and they were both as excited as children. Robson looked at me with mock anger. "You bastard," he said. "You knew this would happen. We just love the record." They agreed to release a single, but on one condition: They didn't want to appear on *Top of the Pops*. I agreed. We had a deal.

On the way home, I played the original Righteous Brothers version of "Unchained Melody" in the car for inspiration. The album then went on to other Righteous Brothers hits, and at some point, the Righteous Brothers' version of "White Cliffs of Dover" came on. I stopped the car in the middle of the street. It had hit me. The record would be released, more or less, on the fiftieth anniversary of V-E Day. Both Robson and Jerome played soldiers on television. We could put "White Cliffs of Dover" on the flip side of the single and probably double the sales.

RCA was nervous. It had been months since Robson and Jerome had sung "Unchained Melody" on the show, and the executives weren't certain the public would still care. I forged ahead anyway. I was absolutely insane with conviction. In those days, successful singles sold about 150,000 units in the first week. We were shipping about 100,000 units, so we were well on course to have a Top 5 single. On the morning of the release, I logged in at work to check on repeat orders—in other words, to see how many additional people wanted the record beyond that initial shipment. The figure was astonishing: It was 1.2 million—

by lunchtime! The song was going to be number one by a mile, my first number one. And while I worried about the week after that, and the week after that, I didn't need to—it stayed at number one for seven weeks. Robson and Green were so thrilled that they even agreed to go on *Top of the Pops,* after all.

The second single we released was another double A side, with "I Believe" and "Up on the Roof." When it came out, I sat down with my head of promotions and asked what the biggest show on television was. *The National Lottery,* he said—it was the show where they drew lottery numbers. So I phoned up the producer of *The National Lottery* and offered him an exclusive opportunity to have Robson and Jerome sing their new single on the show. He agreed. Sixteen million people were watching, and as a result the second single sold 1.1 million in its first week and stayed at the top of the charts for a month. I still had no contract signed with them, even though we'd had two number-one singles—I just hadn't thought about it for some reason—and I began to get nervous that another label would steal them. When I called them up to talk about it, Robson said, "I've been waiting for this call. We're in a hotel. Come and meet us." I was petrified. As it turned out, all they wanted was a fair royalty on the video, which I was more than prepared to give. We all shook hands, and it was then I realized that these guys were two of the most honorable people I had ever met in my life. Almost any other artist would have tried to screw me for another million dollars and I would have had to pay to keep them. But Robson and Jerome were absolutely true to their word.

We put the album out, and it was the best-selling record of 1995. We had the best-selling album again the following year, and at the end of the second album I sat down with them and offered to write a $3 million check to each of them for a third record. Robson smiled. "Simon," he said, "you've made us a lot of money and we've enjoyed it, but we're actors, and this time we're going to say good-bye."

I was disappointed, but it had been an incredible experience. Robson and Jerome were a class act. For starters, they were only in their thirties, but they had all the poise and presence and integrity I could have hoped for. They also made me my first million, which was fantastic, not necessarily because of the money—I didn't think it was enough—but because for the very first time people began to take me seriously. We had managed this massive success without being on the radio, solely with television and canny marketing, and in the end the whole process taught me what was possible for labels if they sold directly to the public. Seven million albums, five million singles, three million videos— and *no radio play!* I still look back on that period as one of the best times of my life. It was innocent and exciting and a very personal success. We went against the prevailing wisdom, made us all millions, and made an absolute fortune for BMG. It was at this point in my career that Radio 1—the U.K.'s largest radio station— labeled me the Antichrist of the music industry.

Despite such phenomenal success, I have to admit to making a few mistakes along the way. My biggest regret was not signing the Spice Girls. Simon Fuller, whom I went on to work with on *American Idol*, became their manager. I was tipped off, even before Simon, that there was a girl band called Spice, as they were then called, looking for a record deal.

I brought up Spice at an A&R meeting at BMG and there were a lot of furtive looks. It transpired that two of the guys at the company were already chasing the deal. So I backed off. Six months later, I bumped into the girls in London and they dragged me into their van and played me their first single. At this point, BMG had apparently backed off the group. I thought the record was sensational. I flew back to the office and got on the phone to Simon, who had recently begun representing them. "If you haven't cut the deal," I told him, "I will literally double whatever anyone has offered."

"I signed the deal yesterday," he replied.

A few months later, the Spice Girls exploded onto the scene with their first song, "Wannabe."

In retaliation I hired the guy who had put the Spice Girls together, Chris Herbert. I told him that if he had done it once, he could do it again. I initially gave him £25,000 and he put together the band 5ive—essentially the male equivalent of the Spice Girls. 5ive went on to sell 1.5 million albums in America and more than ten million records around the world. It made me feel a *little* better.

Luckily for my delicate ego, my next signing was the band Westlife—by far the most successful artists I have signed to date. Westlife, at that time still known as I.O.U., were offered to me by an Irish entrepreneur named Louis Walsh. After they auditioned for me in Dublin, I said to Louis, "You are going to have to fire at least three of them. They have great voices, but they are the ugliest band I have ever seen in my life."

Louis said no.

Two months later he called me, saying he had done what I asked—fired three of the boys and found suitable replacements. So I was the first to see Westlife in their latest incarnation. I thought they were just sensational and signed them on the spot. Westlife—the version I saw then—is a lesson for anyone who thinks they want to make it big in this business, because they had it all: talent, intangibles like the X Factor, but also preparation and focus. When potential artists come to see me for the first time, I consider it a job interview as much as an audition— and as you know from my tales of the British Civil Service, I have the utmost respect for job interviews. When you sit down with a prospective singer or group, sometimes it's in the cold, impersonal light of an office building, and that light tends to expose flaws—including the fact that many artists have no idea what they want to do with their careers. One of the things that impressed me so much about Westlife when we had our first official meeting was how much they knew about the industry. They told me which records they liked and which they didn't, which producers they respected and which they didn't, which writers they admired and which they didn't—and they told me with the confidence and precision of people who had researched the matter. They knew names, and that made all the difference in the world, because it convinced me that this wasn't just a good-looking group of boys with good voices, but rather a determined assembly of ambitious young men who knew their way around the pop market. Normally when you meet a prospective artist they don't know much about the business. This always makes me nervous—if I am about to give you two to three million dollars, I expect you to have a working knowledge of the music industry.

Since 1999, Westlife has had an incredible career and has sold more than 27 million records across the globe. The lads *still* retain the world record of having seven consecutive number-one singles, a record that I believe will be very hard to beat. Coming on the heels of 5ive, Westlife helped me corner the market on British boy bands, which would prove extremely useful when it came to my next project: assisting with the development of the British version of a show that just a few of you out there may be familiar with.

Idol Chatter

In January 2000, I arrived back in London from a holiday in Barbados, and for the first time in my life I was bored. I realized that if *I* was bored, then the record-buying public must be even more bored. I was consumed with the idea of selling records to the public in a more interesting way. Again television was to provide the solution.

Reality television first hit the U.K. that same summer. Versions of *Big Brother* and *Survivor* went head-to-head in the ratings. From day one the press and the public couldn't get enough. Within a few days of both shows airing, the British tabloid press had no trouble filling their pages. Lurid details of the shows often overflowed into the news sections.

In February 2001, I had dinner at Bibendum, a restaurant in London, with Simon Fuller, the former manager of the Spice Girls. We met to discuss the astonishing success of the first music-based reality TV program; called *Popstars,* it had just started on British television. The critics loved it, and the viewing public craved more. The idea behind *Popstars* was to create a new pop band from scratch. The show focused on the whole audition process, selecting the members of the group, and then ultimately teaching the group to record and perform its songs. I thought it was terrific, but I had the feeling it could have been better. I didn't like that the band was chosen two-thirds of the way through the series; it didn't make sense. One minute *Popstars* was reality television, and the next it was just a traditional music show with wannabes (fascinating) turning into actors and actresses (boring). Something was missing. There was no ending. And while the show was having a great deal of success in England, I felt as though it could be improved considerably.

If you were going to make a show of this nature, we figured, then you needed to go the distance, but not overrun the finish line. It made much more sense to have a competition in which one person won—it had more dramatic tension that way—and to end the show with the selection of the winner. Simon was keen to have the public actually choose the winner, and he went on to create the format for *Pop Idol.* Subsequently, both Simon Fuller and I worked hard to develop the concept. We spent months agonizing over every single detail of the show. Finally, after many sleepless nights we both agreed that the concept was ready to be sold to the highest bidder. The first target was a production company called Freemantle, to ask if they'd like to make the program. We met a man named Simon Jones, whom I already knew from industry circles, and he loved the idea and took us in to meet his boss, Alan Boyd. Alan is Mr. Flamboyant—he's hysterically funny and never shuts up. That day he wrote down the ideas for *Pop Idol* on an envelope and still carries it around with him today.

We then went to see Claudia Rosencrantz, who was one of the heads of ITV, the U.K.'s commercial TV network. Two minutes into the pitch, she held up her hand and said, "Stop. I'll take it."

I remember saying to her at the time, "Claudia, what has been shown previously on television is not a real-life audition process. This show will be the equivalent of a musical car crash." We explained to her that it would be brutally honest, the kind of thing that people wouldn't be able to take their eyes away from, leading to an ending that would hopefully split the country. I think Claudia was also particularly enthusiastic about Simon Fuller and me working together; Simon was the most successful music manager in the UK, and I was the most successful A&R man. We had both been auditioning artists in the music business for more than fifteen years, and we instinctively knew that what was being shown on *Popstars* was not representative of what really goes on in an audition room. *Pop Idol* would expose what *really* happens during an audition. This was the going to be the hook of the show, and it was not going to be pleasant.

When it came to choosing the judges for *Pop Idol*, my first choice was Pete Waterman—who may be the only person in this book who gets more mentions than me. Simon Fuller suggested a girl named Nicki Chapman, who worked for him and was one of the top promotions people in the industry, and I also brought in Neil Fox, who's a very well-known radio DJ in Britain. Our executive producers would be three of the best in the U.K.: Nigel Lythgoe (who was also one of the judges on *Popstars*), Kenny Warwick, and Richard Halloway.

We went to Manchester in the north of England to start the auditions and were shocked and delighted to hear that more than 10,000 hopefuls had applied. As we walked into the audition room, I suddenly realized that I hadn't discussed with the other judges what we were going to do in the audition room and how we should react to the contestants. Big mistake.

For the first half hour, extremely conscious of being filmed, we were relatively polite to the contestants. Finally, I took Pete to one side. "Listen to me," I said. "This is a disaster. What is this, camera fright? This isn't what we would normally do in an audition. This is not real. Most of the people who are coming in are crap, and I think we should tell them what we would normally tell them."

Pete polished his little glasses and said, "You're absolutely right, mate." Little did he know.

The next person who came in to audition was absolutely dreadful. And we told him so! There was silence in the room. After the unlucky contestant left, Nigel Lythgoe came up to our desk and said, "Thank you for being yourselves—at last." We'd put the reality back in reality television.

I DON'T MEAN TO BE RUDE, BUT . . .
Sometimes the Record Industry Knows Nothing

I can talk with some conviction about what the public wants from a recording artist. I can say that Kelly was the people's choice or that Ruben was the people's choice. This is only because I know it as a certainty. *American Idol* allowed the public to vote, so we have a clear picture of their tastes. This isn't always the case. In the main, particularly when it comes down to pop music, the industry hasn't got a bloody clue what the public wants. The one thing that people tend to want is authenticity. That can mean many different things, but what made the Spice Girls so successful when they were launched in '94 is that every kid who bought their record believed that the girls had done it all themselves, that they were the ones choosing the records, they were the ones choosing their image. They didn't look as if they had been put together by a record label, even though Simon Fuller had decided everything. *American Idol* has also proven that many of the prevailing models for stardom are wrong. The pop-tart clones that have come on the show haven't gotten very far, generally. Just before we went on the air with the first season of *American Idol,* the head of a major record company told me that, in his opinion, the only thing kids want today is a slut who is seen to be screwing as many guys as possible and looks like she's taken a lot of drugs the night before. Really? I told him, "I have never heard so much bullshit in my life." It turns out, of course, that I was right and he was wrong. What a lot of kids today want is Kelly Clarkson or Ruben Studdard, or Clay Aiken. None of them fit that narrow profile that the executive mentioned, and yet all of them have achieved a certain stardom. And I can promise you one thing: If the music industry and not the public had been voting on *American Idol,* Clay and Ruben would not have made the Top 10.

After the first day of auditions in Manchester, I knew we were onto something. If the day's filming was representative of the rest of the audition process, this was going to be amazing TV. I really believed that this was about as close to a real-life audition as you could get: the good, the bad, the ugly, and the insane. The public would love it. When the second episode aired a week later, I felt we had gotten it right—except for one thing. I had always presumed that the judges would be on screen throughout the show. The producers didn't see it the same way. They decided that after the first set of auditions ended, we judges wouldn't be needed. Wrong. I watched the fifth episode, when we were whittling the field down from a hundred to fifty contestants. Suddenly, there was no confrontation. I knew we had a problem.

I spoke to Claudia Rosencrantz, who agreed that the show didn't work once the judges disappeared. I explained that the producers didn't want us in the show anymore. "We'll see about that," said Claudia. A few days later, we were reinstated and the element of confrontation was restored.

Fine-tuning the show during the first series of auditions made all the difference. *Pop Idol* became a national phenomenon, drawing an audience of more than 13 million. Will Young won the first season; he netted 4.6 million votes and beat the runner-up, Gareth Gates, by a whisker. Both artists were signed to my label at BMG, and their sales immediately reflected the massive popularity of the show. Will Young's debut single sold 2 million copies and stayed at number one in the U.K. charts for four weeks. Gareth Gates also showed that he had what it takes to be a pop idol by selling a million copies of his single "Unchained Melody" in the first week. It was no coincidence that it was the same song that had worked for Robson and Jerome—it's a perennially great song that can't fail if it's performed well—and Gates still holds the record as the second-fastest-selling debut artist of all time.

Equally satisfying was having proved once again the power of television as the most effective and exciting tool for selling millions of records. Ultimately, *Pop Idol* proved that the public would always vote for the artists and songs they wanted to hear—and wanted to buy. For the music business *Pop Idol* was a shot in the arm, and not just in terms of sales. Up till then, people had been forced to listen to whatever A&R men thought the public wanted. At last the consumer had a direct say. I was no longer bored with the music business. Neither was the public.

At that point, I had achieved many of my goals. From the mailroom, I had come a long way. I had more than eighty million albums to my credit, some thirty number-one singles, and a hundred Top 30 singles. But still one thing eluded me. I wanted to have a career in the United States.

The British music industry is often accused by the media of failing to produce British artists capable of cracking the American market. It's true; it is difficult to get foreign repertoire played on U.S. radio. So, even before *Pop Idol* broadcast in Britain, Simon Fuller and I had decided to go to America to see if we could sell the *Pop Idol* concept there.

I was ready. But was America?

Coming to America

When I worked with Simon Fuller on the development of *Pop Idol* in Britain, we knew that the show would eventually go to America. It had to. If you want to create the biggest talent show on earth, there is only one country to do it in: the U.S.A. And let's face it—for decades America has been a driving force behind much of global pop culture. Not to mention the fact that the contestants themselves, these talented young people who had earned the chance to become bona fide superstars, epitomized the American Dream. I may be cynical about many things, but I wasn't cynical about that part of *American Idol,* and I'm still not, to this day. There's something incredibly exciting about taking someone who has talent but limited opportunity and making their talent available to an entire nation. Plus, as far as we knew, we had no competition. At the very least, no one else had thought it through to the degree that Simon Fuller had. Producing the British version had allowed us to iron out the wrinkles and perfect the formula, and he thought that selling this brilliant new TV project to America would be easy.

Just before the first season of *Pop Idol* aired in the U.K., Freemantle had managed to set up pitch meetings with a number of TV networks in America. We decided that we would go in force: me, Simon, and a representative from Freemantle. His name, idiotically enough, was Simon, too: Simon Jones. So it was that three extremely enthusiastic Simons arrived in Los Angeles to touch off a revolution in American television.

I soon realized that this wasn't going to be quite as easy as we'd thought. Our first meeting was with one of the smaller U.S. networks. I can't say which, but it was a network that wasn't doing well at the time, and we figured that they needed a show like ours to jump-start their ratings. Simon Jones and I took the meeting and it was a complete disaster from start to finish. The boss of the network was very polite, but his sidekick, a woman, was a nightmare. I had been selected to make the pitch, and I thought I had done a brilliant job. I had talked up the whole concept of *Pop Idol,* explained the telephone voting, and concluded that the show would revolutionize music and talent, all on American television. When I had finished speaking, there was a terrible silence. It went on for a second, then a minute, then an hour—well, maybe not, but it seemed like an hour.

Finally, and without any emotion whatsoever, the woman just looked at me blankly. "So," she said, "what exactly do you want us to do for you?"

"Actually," I said, "it's more a question of what we could do for you." Another silence followed. This one was even longer. At this point I realized that they just didn't get it, and that there was no sense in continuing with the meeting. Simon Jones attempted to reignite the conversation, but it all fell on completely deaf ears. In the end, we were more or less asked to leave. Going down in the elevator, Simon was glum, but I couldn't stop myself from laughing. The response to the pitch just struck me as ludicrous. I was confident that the concept would be sold to the highest bidder, and that the network we had just met with had lost out on the chance of a lifetime. "This place wouldn't have suited the show anyway," I assured him.

Our second meeting, the following day, was with executives from a major TV network. When we arrived for the meeting, I was dazzled by the size of the company's headquarters. It was more than gigantic; it was the most intimidating place I have ever seen. They kept us waiting in the reception area for almost an hour—not a great sign—and I could see that Simon Jones was getting anxious.

Eventually a young, tired-looking executive emerged and led us into a tiny office in the deepest recesses of the building. A monstrously big building, but a monstrously small office: The three of us were so cramped at the table that our shoulders touched. I started the pitch. I explained *Pop Idol,* which was just about to be broadcast in the U.K. I explained the American Dream. I explained the ins and outs of telephone voting. Or rather, I started to explain. Halfway through that part of my pitch, the executive suddenly held his hand up and said, "No."

"Er," I said. It's rare that I'm speechless. "I'm sorry, but I haven't finished yet. Don't you want to hear the rest of it?"

"No."

"Why not?" I demanded.

"Because it's a music show," he said. He sounded exhausted. I was amazed, and underneath the table I kicked Simon Jones to let him know it. The meeting was awful. The climate was awful. The man was awful. I just wanted to leave. I took one last stab, asking if he really meant no when he said no, if he was telling me, in no uncertain terms, that his company would never buy *American Idol.* "Yes," he said, "I am saying that. It's just not for us, I'm afraid."

"Would you reconsider if the show was a hit in the U.K.?" I asked.

"Unlikely," he replied.

After the first meeting, I had laughed, not because I was keeping up a brave front, but because it had never even occurred to me that the show wouldn't sell. After the second meeting, I sat down on the steps of the huge office building and put my head in my hands. I felt as tired as the executive who had said "No." Simon Jones was despondent, and I had made things worse—not with my pitch, which I thought was good despite the man's negativity, but because I had forgotten to order a car to pick us up. For the first time, the possibility of failure came across me like a chill. What if no one recognized the enormous potential of the show? What if no one understood that American viewers were primed for this kind of experience?

We met with Simon Fuller later that evening. He was utterly dumbfounded by the networks' reaction. He had been the most confident of the three of us about the show's potential in America.

No deal had been done by the time we left Los Angeles.

Back in Britain, meanwhile, *Pop Idol* was starting to be broadcast, and almost immediately it was a hit. I returned from Los Angeles to find that I had a never-ending string of press interviews, television appearances, radio conversations, and so forth lined up. Everyone was interested in the show; it was a phenomenon. At around that time, Simon Fuller told me that he was having promising discussions with the Fox network back in the United States. One afternoon, just as we neared the end of the first season of *Pop Idol*, Simon called me. "I think that Fox is going to take the show," he said.

This time, I was surprised that an American television executive had understood the idea; though I knew it was a brilliant concept, my experience with the two meetings in Los Angeles had soured me. As it turned out, it wasn't an American executive at all. Rather, Fox's interest in *American Idol* came right from the top: from Rupert Murdoch's family. Murdoch, of course, is the owner of the network, the head of a global media empire, and at around

I DON'T MEAN TO BE RUDE, BUT . . .
Other Music Reality Shows Are Miserable

American Idol wasn't the first band audition show, of course, and I have to applaud MTV for putting on *Making the Band*. There's no doubt that it gave all of us ideas. But when I think about those other shows, I mainly think about how poor the talent was. When the WB had *Popstars* with Eden's Crush, they were so awful and the show was such a failure that it hurt us. When attempts were made to sell *Pop Idol* in America, executives worried that it would be another *Popstars*. MTV's *Making the Band* was a far better show, but it gave us O-Town. Now, I actually met O-Town at Clive Davis's house outside of New York. I was having lunch with him, and he was thinking of signing the band. They came to his place that day, and it was his birthday, and they made a kind of presentation to him before they performed with a ghastly rendition of "Happy Birthday." I thought they should have forfeited a contract just for that. I never liked them, though it was probably a smart first signing for Clive at J Records: They had momentum. I think that in general the other shows have a difficult problem. *American Idol* succeeds because of its critical edge. The other shows either forgo that lions-and-Christians element, in which case no one wants to watch them, or they include it and suffer accusations of copying us. The one show that does work quite well, I think, is *Star Search,* which was there long before us and didn't change its formula much when it relaunched after the first wave of reality TV.

that time it was rumored that his thirty-two-year-old daughter, Elizabeth, had told her father all about *Pop Idol.* The show, she explained, was exploding in the U.K., and she was convinced that it would work just as well in America. For all the time we spent trying to convince those gray-eyed, balding, bags-under-their-eyes execs at other companies, it was Elizabeth Murdoch who helped us secure our U.S. deal with Fox. Thank you, Elizabeth. Fortunately, the three main executives at Fox (Sandy Grushmaw, Gail Berman, and Mike Darnell) had already expressed enthusiasm and, I think, would have taken the show regardless—Fox has a young demographic and it was in many ways a natural fit for them.

Right away—I think it was the next day—I got a phone call from America, from Freemantle's U.S. offices, saying that Fox wanted me to come to the United States to help oversee the American version of the show. In fact, they wanted me to be one of the judges. They told me what they were willing to pay; I thought it was reasonable enough. To be honest, I didn't really think too much about it. I was thrilled just to have the show in America, and for a little while, that was enough for me.

But then reality set in. Nigel Lythgoe and Kenny Warwick, who were two of the executive producers on *Pop Idol,* had flown over to America to start working on the series. In the meantime, I went to Germany for a meeting with my bosses at BMG, and we started talking about the global pop market, and how we wanted to position ourselves over the course of the next year or two. In that meeting, it dawned on me that I couldn't judge the American version of *Pop Idol.* For starters, the idea of having to sit through more of those bloody auditions filled me with horror. And then there was the matter of my nationality. While I knew the U.K. record industry very well, I didn't know very much about the American business. So what right did I, as a Brit, have to go to America and judge American talent? As much as I prize opinion, it's informed opinion I value. I hate opinion that stems from nothing but attitude; it's the depth of ignorance. I became adamant—I just didn't want to do it. It's true that I was putting Fox in a tight spot, but they still had about a month before auditions were due to start. I figured they would just replace me with Nigel Lythgoe; he had been the original "Mr. Nasty" on *Popstars* in Britain, and though he was a bit older, I was sure he'd do a fine job.

I phoned up my lawyer. "Tony," I said. "Have we signed a contract for *American Idol* yet?"

"No," he replied.

"Good," I said. "Then get me out of it. Tell them I'm not coming over to the States to do the show." My lawyer called back a few hours later, saying that Fox was not happy with my decision. I'm certain that was an understatement. "Well," I said, "I'm still not doing it." Nigel and Kenny then called, and I explained that I had changed my mind. They both said I was mad; I told them I would call them back.

As luck would have it—luck for all you Americans, anyway—the next phone call I received was from Nicola Hill. Nicola's one of my oldest friends; she has worked in the music industry for years and she's a very, very bright girl. "I'm having a rough day," I said. "I just told the people over in America that I'm not going to do their version of *Pop Idol.*"

I explained my reasons to her, and there was a short pause. "Simon," she said, "I'm going to give you a piece of advice. If you don't do this show, you'll regret it. If it's a hit without you, you'll be pissed off, and if you pull out of it and it isn't a hit, you'll think maybe you could have made a difference. You have absolutely nothing to lose, and as a friend I'm telling you, I think you should do it." Nicola always made sense, and this time was no different. When I hung up with her, my opinion had entirely reversed. See? If someone makes a compelling case, I can change my tune.

All I had left to do was to overcome my doubts about judging American talent, and that was easier than I had thought. I realized that my business was judging singers: Russian, Chinese, Japanese, Greek, even American—it didn't matter. A good singer is a good singer. I phoned Kenny Warwick back, and told him that I had changed my mind. Two weeks later, I was on a plane to Los Angeles to begin the great experiment.

At that point, all I knew about the show for sure was that it was going to be called *American Idol.* I also knew the identities of some of the other judges. One was a guy named Randy Jackson, whom I knew of in business circles as a very successful A&R man with a great reputation. The third judge was Paula Abdul, whom I knew about from her pop career. At that time, the plan for *American Idol* called for four judges, just as there had been on *Pop Idol.* But the fourth judge had not yet been selected.

Nigel Lythgoe was waiting for me at the hotel. As soon as I stepped out of the car, he started bringing me up to speed. "We don't have time to mess around," he said. "We're due to start auditions in two days. I know you'll love Randy and Paula, but we'd like your input on the fourth judge. Can you meet with two of the three possibilities tonight?" I was exhausted—the flight had been eleven hours long—and I begged Nigel for another day. "We don't have any time," he said. "Brian can explain more."

Brian was Brian Gadinski, the American executive producer, whom I met as soon as I arrived at the hotel; along with Nigel and Kenny, he completed the production triad. I liked Brian instantly, for his poise and his sense of humor. Brian, too, was fixated on the issue of the fourth judge. "Do we really need a fourth?" I asked him.

"Well," he said, "Fox is insisting on it, because they've been told not to change the format."

"Fine," I said. "When are we going to meet the first prospect?"

"He's right there," Brian said, and pointed across the lobby.

I looked over and there was Mr. Gray. Everything about this guy was gray: his hair, his skin color, his clothes. When he came to sit with us, I learned that his personality was gray as well. I have since forgotten his name (no surprise), but I do remember that he worked as a music writer in New York—a very, very serious music writer. It was obvious to me that he would hate the show, and that anyone watching the show would hate him—and not in a good way. "Have you seen the British version of the show?" I asked him.

"Yes," he said. "I've seen some tapes."

"What did you think?"

"Well, I think I can add a different dimension to the panel. I believe that music is fundamentally an art form . . ."

As soon as this guy started to talk, I was overcome by the powerful urge to close my eyes and fall asleep. He was like human Valium. I excused myself and took Nigel off to the side. "My God," I said. "He is the most boring human being I have ever met in my entire life. If I have to go back and listen to him drone on about art forms for another minute, I'll die. I'm going upstairs to have a shower. Call me when the other judge arrives."

About a half hour later, post-shower, Nigel called. "We have the other candidate," he said. His voice sounded strange. I went downstairs. This time, instead of Mr. Gray, it was Mr. . . . well, I'm not sure I can even describe him. He was close to fifty years old and had hair down to his waist, or maybe even a little bit lower. He looked like an aging roadie. Everyone around him had expressions on their faces pitched midway between amusement and horror. The second I stepped toward this guy, he leapt up and gave me a vigorous two-handed handshake. "Simon," he said, "I can't wait to start working with you. This is going to be fantastic." I asked him to tell me a bit about himself, and it was as if I had launched a rocket. "My main job is cartoon voices," he said. "But I do everything. I can DJ, I can sing, I'm a session singer, I do jingles. But my main thing, as I said, is cartoon voices." He then proceeded to demonstrate with a medley: a little bit of Popeye, a bit of Mickey Mouse, some Minnie Mouse, some Goofy—it was a complete nightmare. "Think of how much fun I'd be on the road," he said. That was it. I actually couldn't think of anything worse. I shot Nigel a look, and he told the man that we would let him know our decision soon.

After he left, I sat down with Brian and Nigel. "Let's just start off with three judges," I said. Brian reiterated that Fox was determined to keep the British formula intact. "I understand that," I said, "but I would rather do it with just three than work with people like that. I hope to God that the other two judges aren't anything like this. I mean, I have heard good things about both of them, but now I don't know what to think."

"Let's just call it a night," Nigel said. "And tomorrow you'll meet Randy Jackson."

So, the following day, I was introduced to Randy Jackson over lunch, and it was one of those rare occasions in life when, within seconds, you find yourself totally at ease with another human being. The first thing that struck me about him was his personality. "Sunny" didn't even begin to describe him—he could light up any room, no matter what the size—but without being irritating like Mr. Cartoon Voices from the previous night. He was familiar with the show, understood the concept, and on top of all that he was entirely qualified. He had been a successful studio and touring bassist, and he had worked for years as an A&R man with artists like Mariah Carey. I didn't see any drawback to Randy. That didn't happen until later, when we were out on the road, and I came to realize that he was the worst name-dropper on earth. At that first meeting, though, I really warmed to him, and it was a good thing—the first round of auditions was scheduled for the very next day. "You'll meet the rest of the crew tomorrow," Nigel told me as we wrapped up the meeting. "And of course you'll get to meet Paula."

The next morning, horribly early, a car picked me up from the Four Seasons and took me to the auditions. When I walked in, the first people I met were Ryan Seacrest and Brian Dunkleman, the two hosts. This, too, was a part of the formula, lifted wholesale from the British version. The two hosts on *Pop Idol,* Ant and Dec, had been a huge part of the show's success: viewers loved their chemistry with each other, their banter with the judges, their comments to the contestants. But duplicating their effect wasn't going to be so simple. Even before *Pop Idol,* Ant and Dec had been working together for years; they had honed their act very carefully. Brian and Ryan had just been thrown together—and, to make matters worse, they were polar opposites. Brian was a standup comic (allegedly) and, as a result, a cynic. And while it's true that many comedians aren't funny when they're offstage, Brian did them one better—he wasn't funny onstage either. Plus, he didn't even seem as if he wanted to be doing the show. Ryan, on the other hand, was the absolute opposite. He had started as an intern at an Atlanta radio station and moved quickly to Los Angeles where he became a popular DJ, and it was easy to see why. He was good-looking and enthusiastic, maybe too enthusiastic: I used to say that if he had a tail he would have wagged it. He reminded me of the dog in the

Garfield cartoon: always happy with his tongue hanging out. From the start, I was fairly certain that the partnership between the two hosts wouldn't survive, and that Brian was going to end up being the casualty. That turned out to be the case, of course, although I had to wait a whole year to see it happen.

The other obstacle I had to overcome that first day, apart from my concern over Brian, was Paula Abdul. I remember quite clearly walking into the room and seeing her for the first time. "Cute" was my first thought. "Small" was my second. Of course, I was aware of Paula as a singer and a dancer, but I knew nothing of her as a person. She seemed nice enough, if reserved, and early that morning, before the singers started to appear, I sat down with her and Randy to briefly discuss the show. Then the three of us went into the holding room to see the singers lining up to audition. They were clearing their throats, practicing their scales, trying to remember the lyrics of their favorite songs. They were so excited, so full of hope. Little did they know what they were getting themselves into. I don't think Paula knew, either.

Here Come the Judges

When the first singer was ushered into the first *American Idol* judging session, it was a historic moment in the history of American television—and in the history of abysmal singing. He sang and then, mercifully, stopped. He stood there, hopeful. Randy was the first to judge. "Yeah," he said, "that was a little bit pitchy, but you were good, dog. I kind of liked it."

Paula was equally noncommittal: "I loved your audition and I admire your spirit," she said. "I don't know if it's quite the voice we're looking for, but I really like you."

I cleared my throat. "I think that we have to tell the truth here, which is that this singer is just awful. Not only do you look terrible, but you sound terrible. You're never going to be a pop star in a million years." There was total silence in the room.

After the contestant skulked out, Paula turned to face me. "What did you just say?" she said.

"I just told him what I thought."

"You can't talk to people like that," she said.

"Yes I can," I said. "In fact, I just did."

"But this is America."

"Yes. And?"

"And he's just a kid."

"A kid who happens to sing terribly."

"Are you going to carry on doing this?" she said. "He wasn't that bad." She was more stubborn than I had expected.

"Paula," I said, speaking slowly, "he was that bad. And if they're really awful, then I believe we've got to tell them the truth. This is what I do. I'm not doing it to be rude, but I'm the record company here, and he was terrible."

She stopped then, but the next singer was just as bad, and got the same treatment, and the one after that was even worse. It wasn't going well, and Paula was open-mouthed with horror.

After about an hour, I called Nigel and Brian outside for a smoke and a talk. "I think Paula is going to walk," I said. "I can just tell she hates this show and she definitely hates me. I don't think she wants to be associated with something like this. I get the feeling she's too sweet."

Nigel didn't disagree. "But let's keep moving forward," he

said. "Let's at least make it to lunchtime and then we'll see how she feels."

The morning rolled along, but by then the contestants coming in had started to hear about the tone of the auditions from the contestants going out, and they were becoming a bit more combative. After we broke for lunch, I went to talk to Paula, as Nigel had suggested, and I found her backstage, sobbing her eyes out. "Simon," she said, "I can't stay on this show. I didn't realize it was like this. This is terrible."

"Look, Paula," I said. "We're not being vicious on purpose. Both you and I know what the music industry is like, and we have promised the American audience that we're going to portray it honestly. You're out there because you're sweet, and I'm out there because I'm not. It's about striking a balance." It didn't make a dent in her misery. For the rest of the afternoon, she was in pieces.

Then, toward the end of the first day, Nigel and Brian brought around the final option for the fourth judge. Again, I don't remember much about him: His name was Greg, he was a record producer of some kind, and he had a broken leg. We brought back a contestant that we had already judged as a kind of trial for Greg, and he immediately upset the balance between Randy, Paula, and me. He was cliché and unnatural and really annoying. And interestingly, even Paula came up to me and told me that she wasn't happy with him. "I was just beginning to feel comfortable with you and Randy," she said. "I like it with the three of us, I don't like this guy, and I don't think we need him on the show." Thankfully Nigel and Kenny spoke to Fox, and eventually they conceded that we could stick with just us three.

What was interesting after that first day was how completely it eradicated my anxieties about the difference between Britain and America. In short, there was no difference. Just like back home, 90 percent of the people were awful and 10 percent were good. Since 100 percent of the contestants believed that they were somehow destined to be big stars, that meant that 90 percent were deluded. It was an epidemic.

The main difference between English contestants and American contestants is the degree of combativeness they show, especially the women. For example, there was a girl named Tamika who auditioned in Los Angeles. She wasn't very good, and we told her that in no uncertain terms. In response, she told us, also in no uncertain terms, that she disagreed with us, that we were stupid, and that she would prove us wrong. I loved her for that. Auditions are a very difficult, very one-sided process, and nine out of ten times, when you tell a contestant that he or she has no talent, they'll just thank you and slink out of the room. That's why I always encourage them to speak their minds. It's their only chance, and now and again they'll say something that will strike a chord in the judges, or even in the public. In Tamika's case, we aired her audition, and she became something of a folk hero for standing up to us.

We also met a girl in L.A. named Tiffany Montgomery. She was a beautiful girl with an original vocal style, and we put her through, but she was extremely quiet and reserved. I thought her shyness would be a major problem, but Paula saw some potential for stardom in her, and decided to mentor her. That was very nice of Paula, but it had an unforeseen effect: Tiffany became so confident and so convinced of her own abilities that she became a pain in the ass. She changed her name to Ryan Starr, for starters, which is how she was known for the rest of the *American Idol* experience, and her attitude in later phases of the competition left something to be desired. If she was the cream of the crop in Los Angeles, I was worried. This was America, a huge country with a wonderful tradition of superb singers, and the best I had seen was a shy little girl with an okay voice and an identity crisis. "Bloody hell," I thought. "I hope the rest of America's better than this."

The second stop on that inaugural audition tour was Seattle. I had never been there before, and from the start I wondered what they were putting in the drinking water, because it was unquestionably the weirdest group of people I had ever seen: all shapes and sizes of strangeness, but again, little real talent. The only one who made any impression was a guy named A. J. who started off as a break dancer and segued into a performance of "America the Beautiful." Well, it was different. He seemed nice—didn't have a great voice or personality, but he was a standout in a weak field. He wept when we told him he was coming to Hollywood.

When we got ready to leave Seattle, I was feeling a bit depressed about the process. I had expected to find the next

Mariah Carey or Whitney Houston—I really had—but the cities, and the singers, were letting us down. There were too many teen-pop clones, too many young girls who fancied themselves the next Britney Spears or Christina Aguilera, but who misunderstood the appeal of those artists. They tried to be sexy but failed, and their hearts weren't in their performances. It's a good thing that Chicago was next, or else I might have sunken into a permanent depression. The thing I loved about Chicago was that the people were genuine: They had real personalities, if not real talent. In Los Angeles, remember, almost everyone is in the entertainment business in one way or another, and as a result, almost everyone is a professional auditioner. This has the dual effect of making them seem insincere and also of sucking the individuality right out of them. Chicago couldn't have been more different, and it couldn't have come at a better time.

But again, in terms of raw talent, Chicago was very poor. Good personalities don't necessarily make for good entertainers, although they made the auditions quite a bit more interesting. One person whom I remember clearly was a guy named Jim Verraros, who would go on to make the Top 10. Both of Jim's parents were deaf, and he said that it made him sad that they would never be able to hear him sing. When he sang, I wished I were deaf—he was useless. Then one of us, maybe Randy, asked if he signed to his parents when he sang. "Yes," he said, and he sang Nat King Cole's "When I Fall in Love," but signed along with it. It was amazing to watch—technically, he hadn't improved, but it was more engaging and genuine and utterly

I DON'T MEAN TO BE RUDE, BUT . . .
Britney Will Never Be Sexy

If you asked me to describe Britney Spears, I'd say she's pretty. I wouldn't say she's beautiful, and I certainly wouldn't say that she's sexy. At the outset of her career, I believe that most American girls related to her. They didn't feel threatened by her. But years later, when she tried to make herself sexy by wrapping pythons around her neck, she succeeded only in making herself look ludicrous. It's rather like your younger sister putting on makeup for the first time. You just think, "Stop. Don't do it, please." As a result, she has lost much of her core audience. The funny thing about pop music is that, for all its artificiality, it should reflect something real. Avril Lavigne is a good example of this principle. Whether it was her record company or whether it was her management, they got it just right. They understood that there are an awful lot of kids out there who don't want to put makeup on every day, who don't just want to talk about boys or other stereotypical girl things. Girls now are into skateboarding, they're into computer games, and they dress it down. Avril was the updated version of Britney Spears. Her look was right for that moment in time. "Complicated" is a genius pop record, but more important, there were millions of kids all around the world who looked at Avril Lavigne and thought, I really like you because you've got your own sense of style—you're not dressing in silly leather hats and dancing with snakes. There are a lot of girls out there like that. And today, Avril Lavigne is selling ten times as many records as Britney Spears. She's got an individual image and is in touch with the kids, whereas Britney Spears went the other way. When Ryan Starr was in the first season of *American Idol*, she designed her own clothes, she ripped her own dress, she'd slice up her own pair of jeans. She was a pretty girl, and I think a lot of kids voted for her because she did have her own sense of style, she wasn't somebody who needed the stylists, she had her own vision of what she was doing and kids liked her for that. I think the Britney thing is borderline at the moment. I'm going to be fascinated to see what happens with her over the years.

unique. I'm not inhuman, remember: Though he was still a terrible singer, it was a nice story, and we put him through to the next round.

With three cities down, Randy and Paula and I met to assess the talent pool. I complained, as I have said. Randy and Paula were a bit more forgiving. But I couldn't imagine that anyone we had seen thus far would end up captivating the nation and becoming the first American Idol. Then came New York. If I thought things were strange in Los Angeles, Seattle, and Chicago, clearly I didn't know the meaning of the word. New York was absolutely mad; I had never seen such a bunch of lunatics in my life. We had the Mexican midget whom I called Zorro; he had found a lot of pictures of me from *Pop Idol* on the Internet, printed them, and stuck them all over his T-shirt. On the back was a shrine to Paula. He was terrible but hilarious, and I actually wanted to hire him to be the official *American Idol* mascot.

Then, just before lunch, Milk came into the room. You may remember Milk from the introduction—the no-talent Clark Kent look-alike who sang an unhinged version of Neil Diamond's "Sweet Caroline" that included a dramatic reenactment of the Vietnam War? Well, if you don't remember him, you should be grateful. He did his act, which was little more than a joke, and when he finished, I turned to Randy, expecting him to be as thoroughly disgusted as I was. Instead, he said he quite liked him. I was furious. "Fine," I said, "the two of you can judge without me." I stood up and walked off.

Randy followed my lead and walked off as well. That left Paula on her own, and suddenly Randy and I realized that there was some slim chance that she might put him through to the next round. We ran back and dragged Milk out by his legs.

After lunch, Nigel and I returned to the auditions and heard a terrible wailing coming from the makeup room. It was Paula, crazed. "I can't believe that you're letting them make me look like a fool," Paula said to Nigel as we entered.

"What do you mean?" Nigel said.

Between sobs and gasps, Paula noticed me standing there in the doorway. "How could you leave me alone and then come back in and undermine me?" she said. "I need to be able to make the right decisions, but no one lets me make any decisions at all." Nigel explained that we couldn't let her pass Milk along for her own sake, that it would have hurt her credibility. "But we have put funny people through before," she said.

"Yes," Nigel said slowly, "but he went too far." He got

through to her eventually, but the producers decided that Paula should take the rest of the afternoon off to clear her head. That was fine with me and fine with Randy. We went back into the audition room and merrily rolled along. Then, at some point, in the midst of somebody murdering a Stevie Wonder or Whitney Houston song, Paula reappeared. At that point, I really thought the entire show was in jeopardy. The tension was so tremendous, the bad feeling so strong, that I didn't know how we could continue together.

The second day in New York, things eased up a bit, mostly because of Justin Guarini, who just came in and blew us all away. He was attractive, charming, with a good if not great voice, and he knew how to present himself. More to the point: He knew to target Paula, who was instantly besotted with him. He turned her to jelly. At that point, I thought he might win the whole competition.

New York was also noteworthy for the thin-skinned nature of some of the contestants. New York is a tough city, and I'd expected people to take what you said to them standing up; but in some cases it turned out to be exactly the opposite. Two of the people I dismissed as terrible (because they *were* terrible) went and rounded up their friends, and waited outside for me with baseball bats. I didn't know anything about it until the next day, when I was riding up in the elevator and one of the production assistants mentioned it in passing. And people wonder why the judges now have bodyguards.

On the flight to Atlanta the next morning, the tension between Paula and me was horrific. I remember offering Paula an ice cream in the airport and receiving a terse reply delivered through gritted teeth. We traveled in silence. The following day we started the auditions, and that afternoon it all blew up. A contestant came in and gave a truly bad performance. "You've got prospects," Paula said. "With a few singing lessons, I think you could do well."

I turned to Paula and said, "I think you're patronizing this guy. If this was a hundred-meter sprint where you had to run it in eleven seconds to be competitive, he would take five hours. He is so far off the mark, he could take a thousand singing lessons and never be able to do any better than he's doing now. He's wasting his life."

Paula turned to me, and I have never seen her look so furious. "I'm not patronizing him!" she spat back.

"Yes you are," I replied. When the contestant walked out of the room, dejected, Paula followed.

Nigel ran to catch up with her. "We're going to have to sit down and clear the air," he said. "It's not working for you and it's not working for me and it's not working for Simon."

That night, all of us met in Nigel's suite—both producers, both hosts, and all three judges. I didn't have high hopes for fixing things, but I spoke to Paula clearly and honestly. The disagreements weren't personal, I explained, or shouldn't have been. We were judging talent. If Paula wanted to go on being too nice, or what I perceived as too nice, that was her right, but I was going to tell her what I thought of her opinion on camera. And if she disagreed with me or with Randy, she should hold her ground. We weren't actors. We were, essentially, on-screen A&R people who owed it to the audience and the contestants to be brutally honest.

For the first time in the whole process, Paula surprised me. "Okay," she said. "Now it's clear." And from that moment on, although she lost her composure now and again, she was much calmer and more confident.

When you're on the road auditioning, there is nothing more demoralizing than blandness: kids with nice voices, nice smiles, and zero personality. But there is nothing more exciting than discovering a real talent. Which is what happened on the second day in Atlanta, when we first saw Tamyra Gray. The morning went fairly well; we saw RJ Helton and EJay Day, both of whom would go on to be Top 10 contestants, and some others who were good but not great. Then Tamyra walked in and delivered one of the best auditions I've ever heard. Not one of the best *American Idol* auditions, but one of the best auditions, period. To me she was the complete package: She was smart, she was attractive, she had a beautiful voice, she had a calmness about her, and she had presence. It was my first opportunity to give effusive praise, and I gave it. "We're looking for the X Factor," I said, "but you have the Z Factor, because you go beyond X. You are to me what this competition's all about."

Atlanta was also the site of one of the strangest incidents in the entire first season of the show. One of the junior producers came up to me on the second day and handed me a piece of paper. "What is this?" I said.

"Well," he said, "the crew and I have written some more put-downs for you." I was confused and said so. "Put-downs," he said. "You know: insults. Someone writes your lines, don't they?"

"No," I said.

"So you write them yourself?"

"They're not written," I said. "What I say is what I'm thinking. I don't plan in advance." This stunned him. He asked if I was sure I didn't want to take a look at the list. "I am more than sure," I said, "because it's a script, and this has to be unscripted to work properly. I don't want to put myself in the position of reading what you have written, maybe liking it, and then changing what I do so I can say one of your clever lines." He took his list and went back to his friends. Maybe they eventually got some use out of them somewhere else.

Dallas, which followed Atlanta, was disappointing. The room we auditioned in was cramped and depressing. The weather was terrible. Dallas was where we first saw Kelly Clarkson, but there wasn't anything about her that jumped out at us at that point. She had a sense of humor—she could tell that we were bored, and she offered to swap places with Randy so that he could sing and she could judge. But beyond that, she was just a girl with a good voice. None of us picked up on her real talent. Then came

Nikki McKibbin, a very attractive girl who was a bit rebellious and reminded me of Pat Benatar. Nikki made it through, but none of us came away from Dallas with the excitement of Atlanta or New York. Finally, after weeks on the road, we finished up in Miami, where there was a jubilant, last-day-of-school mood. The only person I remember clearly from Miami was Christina Christian, another beautiful girl who gave a decent if unspectacular performance.

We were all happy that we had made it through the process. We were all certain that the show would be a big hit. But overall, I was slightly disappointed. In my mind, there were only two front-runners, Justin and Tamyra, and I would have been happy if either of them went on to win. I thought that Tamyra had a real chance to go on to be an international star.

Back in Pasadena a few weeks later, we met to trim the field of one hundred to fifty. At one point, Paula and Randy and I went into a room to make some initial cuts, and Paula accused us of being sexist. "You're ganging up on me because I'm a girl," she said.

"That's stupid," I said. "You're both Americans and I'm British, but I never argue that you're ganging up on me." Then we both lost it. Really lost it. But as mad as we were, Nigel Lythgoe was just as mad, because the film crew was outside the room, unable to film the fight, which would have made for some fantastic footage. In the end, the argument cleared the air: Paula screamed, I screamed, and Randy just laughed.

During the process, the two people I expected to shine shone again. Tamyra was sensational, and Justin blew everyone away. He was absolutely unbelievable. Not a single person there thought that anyone other than Justin Guarini was going to win the competition; furthermore, Justin himself seemed to know that he was going to win. When he came out to do his final song, "Get Here" by Oleta Adams, the other contestants actually stood up and applauded him as if they were crowning a champion.

I flew back to London to resume my normal life, and within about a week the auditions had faded from my memory. One afternoon, the phone rang. It was Brian Gadinski. "It's a hit," he said.

"What is?" I asked.

"The show, Simon. It aired last night and the ratings were fantastic. I've got fifty radio stations that want to talk to you."

"About what?"

"About you."

"When?"

"Right now."

Half an hour later, I was on the phone with a seemingly endless series of radio DJs, all of whom were saying the same thing. "Simon, the show's fantastic. We love your honesty. We can't believe how bad some of these singers are." Wow, I thought. They actually like me. I could sense there and then that the show was going to be huge.

After that first night when *American Idol* debuted, it just got bigger and bigger. I had to go back to the States to start filming

the final set of shows—what we called "the heats," and at the airport the security guard stopped me. "I'm afraid we may have a
problem with you coming into our country, Mr. Cowell."

"Is there a problem with my visa?" I said.

"No," he said. "I watched *American Idol* last night." Then he
burst out laughing. When I got to the arrivals lounge, people
were screaming my name and pointing. I think I may have heard
some boos as well.

I had only a few short days to settle into my new house in Los
Angeles, after which I was thrown right back into the lion's den.
We were down to thirty contestants, who would perform in
groups of ten; the audience would select three finalists from each
group, and then the judges would add a wild card. These shows
were performed in an empty studio, and that shifted the
ambiance, both for the singers and for us: Those rounds felt cold
and impersonal, and the contestants were at their most nervous.

During the first week, a few of the eventual finalists performed. Tamyra Gray was sensational; Jim Verraros was
appalling; and Ryan Starr sang "Frim Fram Sauce," a weird jazz
number that I had never heard before and hope never to hear
again.

The show was then broadcast on the following Tuesday so
that viewers could vote. On the live Wednesday results show,
Ryan won the round and Tamyra also made it, but somehow Jim
also was voted through. I'll never forget watching him as the
results came in. He did this awful thing where he licked his lips

SIMON SAYS
Final Judgments on the Season One Top 10

EJay Day: EJay was what I call a Six Flags entertainer. In other words, he was no better, and no worse, than any singer you'll find in any amusement park in the United States. And though he had the worst hairstyle I'd ever seen in my life, EJay was a very nice person, and also a realistic one—he was one of the only ones in the Top 10 who knew he had absolutely no chance of winning. Still, he was determined to make the most of his time while he was on national television. Oddly, EJay had a good voice, if you're talking about just pure vocal talent—which, in *American Idol*, you never are. He could outsing Justin Guarini any day of the week, but he just had an average feel about him, and he was one of the first to be kicked out. In fact, the very first time he was featured on the Top 10, he was shown in the opening montage in a ghastly sequined jacket, and he turned toward the camera with a terrible grin on his face. It summed up everything that was awful about him. I remember thinking, your film clip has just killed you. And it did. I fear Six Flags awaits.

Jim Verraros: Jim was lucky, because he had a very good film clip from the early part of the competition; it showed him signing to his deaf parents when he did the audition for me in Chicago. That was an effective tearjerker. On the other hand, he took the criticism very personally and overreacted to a silly degree; he thought I was being particularly mean to him and didn't take it well at all. The other contestants absolutely adored him. Even though he failed as a singer, he could have been a cult leader. He had the other contestants wrapped around his little finger, and whatever happened to him, he was the one who always seemed to create the most emotion. When he was in the Top 10, he was absolutely awful. The other good singers around him exposed him as just an average vocalist. Still, when he left the competition, people were genuinely upset. They really, really liked him. Also, Jim's image changed fairly radically over the course of the show. He was a bit of a geek when we first met him, with glasses and a nerdy wardrobe; later, I remember seeing him when the Top 10 were touring, and he was walking around in leather pants and a ripped T-shirt. He came running up to me. "Simon," he said, "I just wanted to say that I appreciate all the criticism you gave me. I didn't react well to it, but I learned from it. Also, there's something I have to tell you—I'm gay." I burst out laughing because we all knew that from the day we first met him. Jim is somebody who would probably do okay in musical theater but would never ever have a career as a recording artist.

A. J. Gil: We first saw A. J. in Seattle, and he was strange from the start, since he insisted on break-dancing—something that he did so badly that it was laughable. I don't know if he was acting or not, but he was relentlessly nice. Everything about him was nice—too nice, almost in a vacant way. He kept to himself and there was nothing he ever said that was interesting. He was almost like a robot. In terms of talent, A. J. wasn't a terrible singer and he wasn't a good singer. He is, I think, totally unmarketable as a recording artist, but like a robot he'll just keep going. Again, the best thing I can say about him was that he was very nice, very kind. Otherwise, bland with a capital "B."

RJ Helton: RJ got through as the wild-card choice. I think Paula always liked him. We saw him in Atlanta, and more than anyone else he epitomized the phrase "boy band member." He was cute, he had a good but not great voice, and a good but not great personality. If you were scoring him, you'd have to give him a 7 out of 10 on everything—never a 9 out of 10. What was funny was that he really got mad at me when he was in the Top 10. He thought I was giving him a hard time and that I was being personal about it, and I wasn't. I just wanted to make a point, and he was an excellent example: He was never going to be a huge solo artist because he lacked that connection with an audience. He didn't have the X Factor. He didn't have charisma. His mother, on the other hand, was hilarious. She hated my guts. In fact, I could actually feel her eyes boring into the back of my head like laser beams whenever I was judging the final shows. And if ever I passed her in the corridor, she would stop and give me this threatening look. It's a shame that RJ took things so personally, because he had a platform as a result of the show. If I were in his shoes, after *American Idol* I would have brought in three or four other guys and put together a vocal harmony band, using the show's success as a catalyst for the group. When he was eventually kicked out of the competition, he made a little speech in which he pointedly thanked Randy and Paula for all their help and ignored me. But I think he missed the point. The show gave him a calling card and taught him that he wasn't going to make it as a solo artist. That should have pointed the way to a band career. But he didn't have the self-awareness to use his own particular talents to his advantage. He had a lot of growing up to do.

Christina Christian: Christina was one of the Miami contestants, and she was very cute—very, very cute. I said on the show that I had a bit of a crush on her, which isn't really true; while she was adorable, she was too nice for me. Her problem was that as a beautiful, slim African American singer, she was basically competing with Tamyra, and while Christina was a 7 out of 10, Tamyra was a 9 out of 10. Sadly, Christina never really showed her true personality on the show. When I saw her weeks after she was kicked out, on MTV in New York, she was great fun, witty, and even a little bitchy. It was a shame, I thought, that she couldn't show that part of her personality on the show. Rather, she was just seen as a pretty girl with a pretty voice. If she's lucky, she may end up as a television host somewhere. There was talk of her signing a deal with Sony, but I never would have signed her. In three years, no one will remember her. You may have forgotten her already.

Ryan Starr: In a weird way, Ryan remains one of my favorite contestants ever on *American Idol*. First of all, she was at odds with herself. She was cripplingly shy when we first met her, but Paula really took her under her wing and gave her a lot of confidence. The change was extraordinary. In fact, she believed in herself enough to change her name in the middle of the competition from Tiffany Montgomery to Ryan Starr. She put together her own image, designed her own clothes, and in the end it transformed her from a shy, awkward little girl to a very sexy girl. The problem with her, ultimately, was that she wasn't smart enough to know what kind of music would have suited her. She could have been a latter-day Britney Spears, but she saw herself as Chrissy Hynde or Pat Benatar. One of the worst performances I ever saw was one of hers—a truly awful rendition of The Kinks' "You Really Got Me." It was like watching ritual hara-kiri; she just fell apart completely in front of thirty million people. It was unspeakably horrible. When I told her so in no uncertain terms, she accused me of not liking rock music, and I said, "I love rock music when it's sung in tune." She had a nice pop voice, nothing too impressive, like Britney Spears or Kylie Minogue, but she saw herself as a rock belter, a Janis Joplin or something. Which she wasn't. The one thing she did have going for her was that she had the most gorgeous aunt. God, she was sexy, and I was desperate for Ryan to stay in the competition so the aunt would stay around. In the end, the transformation did genuinely strange things to her. While lots of the kids were happy simply for the exposure, she wasn't. Toward the end, in fact, she was downright bitter. When she came back onto the show after she was eliminated, she sat behind Tamyra, who was singing, and she made faces and mocked Tamyra during the performance. I hear now that she's got her own clothing line. I'd be amazed if it ever took off. Like RJ, I think she's one of the ones who blew her chances.

Nikki McKibbin: When we saw Nikki in Dallas, we liked her because she was an individual, with shocking red hair and the most beautiful eyes I've ever seen in my life. They were literally cat's eyes, just hypnotic. Even so, we were all amazed that she made it through to the top three. I think she was perceived as a bit of a rebel, and that helped her with the voting. But let's be honest: Anybody who is really a rebel wouldn't enter a competition like *American Idol*. *American Idol* is not rock-and-roll. I call people like Nikki a sheep in wolf's clothing. Still, the minute Nikki made the Top 10, I made it quite clear that vocally she had no right to be there. She was responsible for some absolutely appalling performances throughout the show. The only time she got it right was when there were four people left—she delivered a great performance and beat Tamyra Gray, who was having an off night. But like some others, she didn't use the show as she could have. What she should have done, as far as I'm concerned, is resigned halfway through, announced that the show wasn't right for her, and that she wanted to start a band. She would have been headline news and everyone would have respected her. She really took it personally that I'd put her down on the show and never spoke a word to me after the competition was over. I saw her weeks later at an airport. She didn't have any makeup on, she looked exhausted and miserable, and she was clutching a teddy bear. She didn't seem to be enjoying her life. I hear she's running a karaoke club again.

Tamyra Gray: When everything is said and done, Tamyra will probably be my all-time favorite *Idol* contestant. In hindsight, however, you could look back and see how she unraveled as the show went on. There were, I think, two things that went against Tamyra. One was the fact that she just happened to arrive at a time when artists like Whitney Houston and Mariah Carey just weren't selling records anymore. If she'd have been in the competition at the time those artists were huge, she would have been a superstar. But she missed the moment for that kind of vocalist. The other thing that worked against her was that she was so polished and perfect that the audience may have stopped rooting for her. People didn't call in and vote for her because they assumed she was already the front-runner. She just had that air about her. Still, it's hard for me to forget her performances: She sang a Dionne Warwick song, "A House Is Not a Home," and a Tina Turner song, "Fool in Love," and both were just incredible acts of showmanship and technical mastery. Tamyra was also very warm and kind; she was careful not to ingratiate herself or get too close to the judges in a way that would piss off the others. But after the show ended, she was the only one who picked up the phone and called to see how I was doing. I haven't spoken to her in a while, but I can't say enough good things about her. I really hope that in the future she gets what she deserves out of this business, because she is a class act.

Justin Guarini: I like Justin; as the competition proved again and again, it is very hard not to. He was like a puppy dog who just wanted to be loved. From the start, he was very charming without being ingratiating. Interestingly, if Justin had been in the English competition, he would have had a better shot, since U.K. radio supports a different kind of recording artist. In America, it was tougher because Justin was one of those people who was good at everything but not fantastic at anything. He is a good dancer but not a great dancer, a good singer but not a great singer, a good actor but not a great actor. He's just good. The thing with Justin boiled down to this: He could end up as a huge star, or he could end up singing at weddings. He was borderline. From a backstage perspective, one of the things that elevated Justin was his parents. His birth father was one of the best characters of the show. On the night of the final, I went up to him and said, "Let me ask you something. I have watched you all night long, and you have been cheering for Kelly as much as you cheered for your son. I don't understand that." He answered, simply, that he wanted them both to do well. He must be nuts.

Kelly Clarkson: I remember that Pete Waterman, one of the judges on *Pop Idol*, once made a prediction about the British competition. "The winner won't be the flashy, controversial, good-looking showboater," he said. "It will be the person sitting quietly at the back of the room who's got the talent, and who knows they've got the talent, who will win this competition." That's exactly what happened with Kelly. She was not on the radar until she made the Top 10, and that's when she came into her own. From the start, it was apparent that she had a great voice. But she had never found the right outlet for it. Before *American Idol*, she was there, wanting to sing, able to sing, and for whatever reason—whether it was her image or poor luck—

she never got the break that she deserved. She had hooked up with a record producer but nothing was happening, and she was working as a cocktail waitress. Before the show, she was very close to giving up her dream. You could say that the show transformed her, but it's more accurate to say that it brought out what was already there. Kelly knew that singing was only part of the competition, and that the way she acted when she wasn't singing was just as important. Whenever the contestants would say good-bye to a departing singer, and start crying, she would be right there in the middle of it all. When one of us complimented her onstage, she had this little trick of looking humble. Oddly, I didn't get to know her very well during the competition. One afternoon, when there were about five contestants left, I tried to talk to her. I was having a cigarette and she was on her mobile phone, and I walked over and said, "Kelly, I think you're going to do great in this competition and I'm very keen to know what type of music you personally like." She thanked me but said that she didn't feel comfortable talking to me because I was a judge. I thought it was a bit strange, but it also showed me how determined she was to stay focused. As it turned out, she was unquestionably the right person to win. We needed somebody who had the potential to be a big star both in America and around the globe, someone who was focused, who was talented, and who was a hard worker in every respect. Since the show, I've seen her confidence grow. Now, when you bump into Kelly Clarkson, you know that you're in the presence of a star.

and then let his tongue loll out of his mouth; it was just revolting. Jim's victory put me in a bad mood that lasted until the next heat—I spent the whole week worrying that we had placed this competition in the hands of America, and that America might choose the contestants with sympathetic stories—like Jim—over those with the real talent. What if someone like Jim won? It would be a disaster.

In the second heat, RJ Helton performed. He didn't sing particularly well, and I told him that I had expected more from him and that it was a weak performance. I also complained about the general standard of the singers left in the competition. Then a voice came at me from my side: "You can't talk like that to people." I sighed, but this time it wasn't Paula. It was Randy. Randy? I stood my ground, and then out of the blue he exploded. He was really mad. Unbelievably, he then stood up and squared off against me. It was like facing Mount Kilimanjaro, if mountains had bad moods. It occurred to me that he might actually punch me in the face on network TV. For the first time I was scared, but apparently I was the only one. Paula was smirking. And then she chimed in. Great! The contestants were watching excitedly. Backstage, Nigel Lythgoe and the Fox executives were rubbing their hands together with glee. "Fantastic, Randy's going to knock Simon out." Of course, Randy eventually calmed down—he is a reasonable man—and even offered me an explanation backstage. "Forget it," he said. "I just lost my temper. I've had to put up with you over the last few weeks, and

I just got fed up. Now I feel better." I was relieved; it doesn't pay to get on the wrong side of Randy Jackson. In the end, those heats yielded three more finalists: Kelly Clarkson and Justin Guarini, who performed wonderfully, and A. J. Gil, who was just okay.

The next week was completely predictable. Christina Christian won the heat, and Nikki McKibbin and EJay Day also got through. The week after that, we had what we called the wild-card show; this was a fourth heat show in which we brought back six people from the first three shows and gave them a second chance. One of the people we brought through was RJ, who had been the cause of my argument with Randy, and that night he outsang everybody. He sang Stevie Wonder's song "Lately," and he sang it very well. When we told him he was going through to the final ten, he was absolutely gobsmacked. At last we had our final ten.

Down to
the Wire

My first thoughts on the Top 10 from season one of
American Idol were not charitable ones. At that point, they seemed
like a dull group of singers—and, for that matter, a dull group
of people. As a record label executive, there were then only two
people who interested me at that stage: Tamyra Gray and Justin
Guarini. Only two, that is, until we did the first live show and
Kelly Clarkson walked out and opened her mouth. I turned to
Randy with my eyes wide and said to him that I thought she was
going to walk away with the competition. Randy just smiled an
enormous smile and said, "This time you're right."

The popularity of the show had taken all of us by surprise,
and in Paula's case it resulted in her reverting to an earlier diva

state. Her entourage grew to at least a dozen people, and she became happier and more confident. At this point, even though I was still winding Paula up, we were getting along overall. Against my better judgment, I had come to appreciate her sunny outlook and her unique perspective, and I think she had begun to like me. And no question, she had a crush on me. But there was an unforeseen consequence to her renewed confidence, especially as the live shows got longer and more spirited and the arguing among the judges increased. After the second round of heats, I heard a rumor that Paula had hired a gag writer to help her deal with me. I didn't believe it, but sure enough, during the show, Paula turned to me after some comment and delivered this masterpiece: "Your father must have breast-fed you as a child." What the hell did that mean? I was dumbfounded, along with everyone else in the studio. She went on: "The only high you'll ever get is if you smoke your own T-shirt." Unfortunately for her, she had somehow managed to hire the worst gag writer in Los Angeles. I had no response—what could you say to something that idiotic?—but Paula looked like the cat that just ate the canary, because she felt she had managed to get one over on me. The next day, the Fox executives called us in and asked what the hell was happening. "Well," Paula said, "Simon's so rude to me that I need to be able to answer him back." I agreed, but I told her she didn't need any help, at which point she promptly denied hiring anyone to help her. I rolled my eyes at that, as I frequently did when she spoke. "See?" she said. "That's the kind of rudeness I'm talking about."

If the live shows changed Paula's behavior into something slightly bizarre, they energized other members of the cast and crew. The results shows, in particular, were electric: The audience had the scent of blood, as though they were a Coliseum crowd in gladiator days. Those shows also elevated Ryan Seacrest. From the start, he was one of the hardest workers on the team; he sometimes put in twenty-hour days without complaining. The deeper we got into the heats and the closer we got to the finals, the more Brian Dunkleman faded into the background and the stronger Ryan's presence became.

The week the finale was broadcast, I went to one of the best parties of my life, along with Ryan and Randy, at the Playboy Mansion. The dress code was lingerie for the women and pajamas for the men. A beautiful house with fifteen hundred girls running around in underwear, a few guys in pajamas: Hugh Hefner is a genius.

By this time Ryan, Randy, and I had become good friends. Behind the scenes, Randy did more than people know. He was the person who constantly reminded me that it was a reality show, and that we were on the show as record executives. He was also a vital middleman whenever Paula and I got on each other's nerves, which was roughly five hundred times per week. And Randy and Ryan weren't the only ones I socialized with. There was Mike Darnell, one of the Fox producers whom I love—a tiny man with the worst permed hair you've ever seen and ripped jeans—but a genius of reality TV (he would later create *Joe*

Millionaire). And, of course, Nigel Lythgoe, the *Popstars* judge, with whom I had a more combative but no less rewarding relationship, and Kenny Warwick. At that point in my life *American Idol* was a happy place to be. The show was going through the roof and we were all getting along, more or less.

For all the parties and the public appearances, the effects of fame weren't entirely apparent to me until my first appearance on *The Tonight Show with Jay Leno*. When I walked out onto that stage and sat down next to Jay, I felt as though I had really accomplished something in America. And Jay was one of the nicest people I have ever met; in fact, he's nicer offstage than he is onstage. He bothers to come to your dressing room and have a real conversation. He sits down with you. He genuinely wants to know about your life. By the time you sit down on camera, you feel as if you have known him for ten years. The only other person as genuine and friendly was Oprah Winfrey. And I really liked Howard Stern—he was a great guy, and very funny.

Everything was going extremely well as the first season drew to a close, and I was sure we were going to have a big finale: Tamyra Gray versus Kelly Clarkson. I had even spoken to Fox about designing posters that depicted the last episode as a big boxing match, an Ali–Frazier situation. Then Tamyra went out and gave the two worst performances she had given during the show's entire run. She looked nervous and sounded only mediocre. Nikki McKibbin followed her and gave the performance of her life. I still felt it wouldn't matter because Tamyra had been so consistent throughout. We opened up voting, closed

I DON'T MEAN TO BE RUDE, BUT . . .
Tamyra May Have Been Too Good

When Kelly Clarkson walked in, it was her talent but also in a weird way her normality that attracted our attention in the first place. If you look at Kelly versus Tamyra Gray, there was a strange dynamic at work. Tamyra was one of the most polished artists I've ever seen in my life. Everything about her was immaculate—her hair, her makeup, her poise, her elegance, her clothes, her choreography, her vocals. She was as close to perfection as you could possibly get, and yet the public didn't really embrace her. I think that they viewed her as too good, and thought that she didn't need their help.

the polls, and went home. The next night, I was prepared to say something vaguely sincere to Nikki about how she had improved greatly. Then Ryan opened and read the results: Tamyra was out of the competition.

I'll never forget it. I was horrified, I just couldn't believe it. I thought it was the wrong decision. Paula was devastated, Randy was devastated. Even Nikki, to her credit, was downcast because she knew she didn't deserve to be in that group and she had absolutely no chance of making the final.

While viewers and contestants alike continued to obsess over how the voting would proceed from that point onward—

Tamyra's departure had taught us that nothing was set in stone—we had to turn our attention to other matters. The real point of *American Idol* was, and had been from the start, the single. We wanted to create a pop star, and that meant that we had to have a song ready to release very quickly after the competition finished. As a result, the week leading up to Tamyra's surprise departure had been spent recording with the four finalists. The two songs that they each sang were one that I had commissioned called "A Moment Like This," which I thought typified what the *American Idol* experience was all about, and another that Simon Fuller had commissioned titled "Before You Love." We decided to make it a double A side single. I turned up at the studio only to find that none of the artists wanted to sing "A Moment Like This." Nikki was exhausted and emotional; she knew she wasn't going to win. Justin, too, felt like it was a waste of time.

Even Kelly loathed the song. "Kelly," I said, "before the show, you were working as a cocktail waitress, and now you're on the brink of this huge victory." I told her to read the lyrics of the song, which said, "Some people wait a lifetime for a moment like this." I explained that the song had been written with the show in mind, and that she could express her own experience through the music.

She went straight in to record it.

The next week on the show, the energy levels were still low. Tamyra's departure had shocked the remaining contestants, and Justin and Kelly gave lackluster performances. They were coasting. Nikki was voted off, as we all knew she would be, and suddenly we had our finalists: Justin and Kelly. I was disappointed, still thinking about what might have been if Tamyra and Kelly had been facing off.

The final episode was a two-part show spread over two nights: the performances and then the results. The three judges turned up at the Kodak Theatre only to be told by Nigel that we wouldn't be sitting in the normal judges' row. Instead, they were moving us to the absolute top of the theatre, so high up we would look like tiny pinpricks. I thought it was stupid. We had been a part of the show throughout, and on the final night we weren't even allowed to speak. Backstage, Justin looked resigned, and Kelly looked as if she were going to be rehearsing an acceptance speech. She was glowing. Justin came out first, sang poorly, and Kelly came out and cinched the victory—to say it was one-sided is an understatement. It was anticlimactic, if I'm being honest. The irony is that I believe we—the judges—would have added to the drama that night. The performances without the critique didn't work, and I think we would have heightened the appeal of the show.

The following night was the results show. America does glitzy events better than any other country. It was like the Oscars, with a long red carpet, searchlights in the air, thousands of people lining the streets, and more than one hundred film crews. It made me smile to think back on the finale of *Pop Idol,* which had been held at a place called Fountain Studios in North London, which is one of the worst parts of the city. I remember standing outside Fountain Studios in the freezing cold as rain poured down on nine fans, one TV crew, and a half-dozen umbrellas. That night, as *American Idol* ended, I saw clearly what was so American about it: It was the scope, the excitement, the glamour. And the fact that there were twenty-six million people watching.

Finally, it came down to the moment we had all been waiting for, or pretending to wait for. When Ryan announced that Kelly had won, I wanted only one thing to happen. I wanted Justin to show some disappointment or competitive spirit. He didn't. Instead, he jumped for bloody joy. That made no sense to me. This was a winner's competition, and it stood to reason that the person who lost would be, at least for a moment, unhappy. At least Kelly had the intelligence to look slightly surprised even though she obviously knew she was going to win.

Up in the nosebleed judges' seats, Paula turned to me and Randy and said, "Guys, this has been an amazing experience. I have loved working with you." And then she kissed us. The crowd below us was going wild. All I kept thinking was that the show had succeeded, that Fox had picked it up for the next season, and that as a result, in four weeks I had to start the process all over again.

Of course, before I could close the book on the first season, there was one absolutely crucial thing left to do. I had to forget all the hype, the ratings, the coverage, and wait on the success of the single. Steve Ferrara at RCA oversaw the production of both singles, and he worked twenty-three hours a day throughout this period. Without a hit single, the entire show meant nothing.

And it wasn't easy to sell a single either; at that time in America, the singles market was worse than moribund.

RCA sent Kelly's single, "A Moment Like This," out to radio stations a few weeks after the show had ended, and it snuck into the lower reaches of the charts: Top 100, but nothing spectacular. Then it went on sale, and within the week it had jumped all the way to number one, one of the biggest jumps in *Billboard* chart history. It went on to sell more than a million copies. For Simon Fuller and me, this was the moment when we could finally relax. If the single had stiffed after six months of hard work on the television series, we would have lost a tremendous amount of credibility for future seasons. We had to prove to the people who were watching that *American Idol* wasn't just a talent show but the gateway to a real career.

The single's success had a real impact on my career. As a record producer based in England, I was trained to think of America as the ultimate market: British music executives are always trying to succeed in the States with British artists. When I started as a judge on *American Idol*, it was because I had a slightly different idea: I wanted to succeed in America with an American artist. When I first sat down with RCA Records at the beginning of the process and told them that they could sell a million singles by the winner of the competition, they looked at me like I was out of my mind. So with Kelly's record sitting atop the charts, with the reputation of the show secured—and my own reputation improved—I was finally able to turn my attention to the second season of the show.

9

Second Time Around

In the six weeks or so between the end of the first season of *American Idol* and the start of the second, the show was everywhere. America couldn't get enough of it. Kelly and Justin were stars. Even Paula, Randy, and I were on magazine covers. The second season brought two other changes, one good and the other bad. The good news was that Brian Dunkleman wasn't coming back, which meant that Ryan would be the only host. This decision, of course, was long overdue, for one simple reason: Brian Dunkleman was an idiot. His behavior on *American Idol,* the way he acted throughout the first season, will go down in history as one of the great blown opportunities in entertainment history. From the start, he had lost the plot, and he was more concerned about what his out-of-work actor friends thought about him selling out than he was about developing a good rapport with the producers, the judges, the contestants, and even the audience. Throughout, he behaved in this slightly contemptuous way—he held himself back, as if to signal his two or three friends who were watching television that he didn't respect the show. And backstage, he was impossible to talk to, distant in every way. I remember that once I tried to sit him down and set him straight. I said, "You're going to blow this. You're taking this too seriously. Lighten up and look like you're having fun. Also you need to spend more time with Ryan to have better chemistry with him. When you're on TV it looks to me like you absolutely hate him, and if I'm picking up on that, so is the audience." He didn't listen. He never listened.

The bad news was that the producers had decided, at long last, to add a fourth judge. The fourth-judge issue had been a thorn in our side since the beginning, and while I didn't mind in principle, I wasn't pleased with the choice. They had picked a young woman named Angie Martinez, who was a DJ in New York and a hip-hop artist.

Paula, Randy, Ryan, and I all turned up in Detroit for the first set of auditions. It was like a reunion after a summer vacation. In the midst of that, we were introduced to Angie. I had expected her to be quite fiery, but instead she was this quiet little girl sitting in the corner. She had never seen the show before, and didn't really know what she had gotten herself into. I gave her one piece of advice: Be yourself. As it turns out, it was the worst advice I could have given.

I had high hopes for Detroit, given that it was the home of Motown. I thought we would get a different kind of artist. We did: The contestants were absolutely useless. Not a single good singer or performer came through Detroit. In retrospect, we may have been victims of our own success. Because the first season had been such a sensation, more than seventy thousand people turned out for the second season. Well, of course, there was no way we could actually see seventy thousand people. Instead, we had to send producers out in advance to narrow down the field. They had found their own favorites, and sometimes we agreed and sometimes we didn't.

But if the contestants were bad, Angie was worse. She didn't say a word the entire time. I take that back. She said one word: "yo!" After about an hour, I realized that she was incredibly uncomfortable with the judging, a hundred times more uncomfortable than Paula had ever been. She was compromised by the fact that some of the kids knew of her work and that she had a record coming out herself. Whatever the reasons, she was hopeless as a judge. Add to that the fact that for all our squabbles, Paula, Randy, and I had established a rhythm that was disrupted, and not productively, by Angie.

Later, I went for a drink with Nigel Lythgoe. After a few minutes of small talk, I told him my real concern. "I have serious doubts about Angie," I said.

"Why?" he said.

"Isn't it obvious?" I said. "It's not working."

"Well, Simon," he said. "I understand what you're saying. But you've just met her. Don't you think she deserves more of a chance?" I protested, but he wore me down and eventually convinced me to wait another day.

I wish he hadn't. The second day was even more dismal than the first. Angie was so lost and so quiet that I found that I was having a hard time disagreeing with her, as was Randy. As a person, she was perfectly nice, but as a judge she was awful. The rest of us couldn't be ourselves, and if that element was lacking, then the whole show was in jeopardy. And the talent in Detroit—or the conspicuous lack of it—did nothing to cheer us up. It occurred to me on that second day that maybe the first season was like a lightning strike, and that we wouldn't be able to duplicate its success. Maybe the contestants would be too careful and self-conscious. Maybe the audience would lose its patience. Maybe Fox would make us keep Angie Martinez.

We flew to New York, the second city on the tour, in a somber mood, and things just got worse from there. We ended up holding the auditions in a terrible hotel room that was small and claustrophobic—a ten-by-ten cell with a carpet that I couldn't look at without getting dizzy. All morning long, we didn't see a single decent singer, and Angie wasn't getting any better. By lunchtime, I had had enough. I told Kenny and Nigel that this was a major problem, that they had a judge who was so uncomfortable she couldn't do her job. They agreed. As it happened, she was feeling the same way, and she went to them and asked to be removed from the show. There were reports at the time that Paula had pushed her off the panel in some sort of catfight, but that couldn't be further from the truth. From the beginning, Paula had always complained that Randy and I made her feel outnumbered, and she quite liked the idea of having another girl with us on the road. As it transpired, Nigel and Kenny simply came back after the break and told us to continue on. Angie wasn't around, and she wasn't missed, and from that point on we picked up the thread of the previous season. We became more animated, and fortunately the contestants got better, too.

The first one to catch our eye was Frenchie Davis, a big black woman with her hair dyed blond. She was calm and serene but had a little smile on her face, as if she knew something that we didn't. Which she did. She knew that she could sing, and the second she opened her mouth we knew it, too. She was absolutely stunning, and the three of us turned to one another and said, "This girl's going to win the competition." She was that good. Frenchie told us that she had made it to the auditions only because her college had bankrolled her trip. She had people who believed in her, and she believed in herself as well; when we told her she was coming through to the next round, she didn't even blink. She knew what she had.

I thought Frenchie was an interesting addition to the competition: She was a big girl, at least two hundred fifty pounds, and she seemed to come from an earlier era, the late-disco period that produced the Weather Girls, Jocelyn Brown, and other big, brassy divas. At that point, it occurred to me that the second season might be considerably different from the first, and that was an exciting notion. The New York auditions also gave us Julia DeMato, a hairdresser from New Jersey. She had a good voice and a kind of negative charm: To be more precise, she had charisma, but there was something dark about her and a little pessimistic. Still, all of us liked her enough to pass her through.

In New York, I also started to notice that the first season had impacted the contestants' view of the show and the judges, and that this was taking a toll on their performances. The first time around, no one had heard of me or Randy, and they may or may not have known Paula. During the second-season auditions, however, contestants came into the room like they were having an audience with the Pope. Almost every single one of them froze up terribly. Nigel spoke to us about this problem, and he decided that the three judges should walk into the holding room each morning and introduce ourselves. We gave a little pep talk that broke the ice. I told the contestants that the most important thing to me was that they show their spirit. If I told them they were awful, I didn't want them to take it lying down. I wanted them to stand up for themselves. When we told people that they weren't going any further, I wanted them to show some self-respect. It ultimately helped a little, but 90 percent of the people we told were terrible still said, "Thank you very much."

The only one who didn't appreciate the more combative contestants, predictably, was Paula. She had kissed me good-bye at the first-season finale. She had been glad to see me at the second-season kickoff. But as the new season got under way, it was clear to me that we weren't going to get along any better this time out. Like so many artists, Paula was a mix of confidence and insecurity. She worried that *American Idol* was a boys' club, and that her remarks were going to be edited to make her look like an idiot. That seemed like a silly concern to me; Nigel and Kenny had always promised to protect the integrity of the judges. And they had. But it was clear that she was tense, and I have always been a little sadistic in this regard—if I sense that someone else is jittery, I'll take advantage of that. Even by the second day in New York, I knew that the relationship between me and Paula wasn't going to be very good.

There was also the strange matter of her growth spurt. I remember sitting in Detroit, thinking that something was strange, but that I couldn't quite put my finger on it. In New York I realized what it was. Paula was higher up than me and Randy. I glanced down and saw that she was sitting on about four pillows. Obviously, some genius had told her that the best way to feel more confident with me and Randy was to appear taller. When she went out to the bathroom, I got one of the runners to get me and Randy five pillows each. When she came back in, we were all on pillows, and Randy and I were towering over her again. We were ridiculously high up over the tables. This continued throughout the competition, as did my habit of lowering her chair when she was out of the room. So I was elated when I learned that she wouldn't be making the trip to Atlanta, the next city, because she had to work on a film. I had loved Atlanta the first time around, and I figured that I would love it even more without Paula there.

The first night in Atlanta, Randy and Ryan and I went to a strip club and had a great time. The girls were gorgeous, we were given the best table in the house, and I could smoke, which is, unfortunately, unusual in America. Ryan was, as always, Mr. Competitive, and he was counting how many girls approached him versus how many approached me. Most of them came up to me, which put him in a bad mood, which put me in an even better mood. I love watching Randy in those situations; he's married and he loves his wife to pieces, and as a result he just sat in the middle of the group like a Buddha, with a huge smile on his face. It was a great way to start our time in Atlanta.

The auditions began the next morning, and I remember two things about the Atlanta talent that second time around. The first thing I remember is Clay Aiken. As I said before, the talent the second year was different. We were getting less of the kind of singer that dominated the first season of *American Idol*, the bratty girls who had been onstage since they could walk and wanted nothing more than to be the next Christina Aguilera or Jessica Simpson. Instead, we were seeing talented people who wouldn't normally enter a talent competition, good amateurs rather than bad professionals. Frenchie was a perfect example.

We hadn't had a particularly great morning when Clay walked in. I formed an impression of him immediately, due in part to his awful hair, his thick glasses, and the abysmal clothes he was wearing. I wouldn't have been surprised to see him pull a laptop computer out of a bag and announce that he was designing his own Web site. He was just a geek through and through; I remember thinking that if we put him on the front cover of a teen magazine, it would go out of business. He was nice enough but really a complete mess. Then he started singing, and all of that was forgotten. When he finished his audition, he stood there, pleased with himself, but he was very nervous. "Well," I said, "you don't look like a pop idol, you have to admit." He nodded. "But, God, you're a really good singer," I said. "What do we do with you?"

"Put me through," he said. So we did. Randy felt exactly the same way about Clay; we agreed that there was an aura about him, something unusual. He stuck in our minds, and that alone was a tremendous achievement—when you see a hundred singers a day, it's amazing if you can remember even a handful of them.

Then somebody else walked into the room whom I'll remember for as long as I live—though for a very different reason. His name was Keith, and he was wearing a weird green sweater. His hair was wild and he had a strange, vacant expression in his eyes. I asked him why he was here, and he told me confidently that he was the best undiscovered talent in America. He then announced that he was going to sing "Like a Virgin" by Madonna. Oh . . . my . . . God! To say that he was awful was an understatement—I had never heard anyone sing this badly in my life. He was so bad that I heard a crash in the middle of the audition and looked to the back of the room to see that one of the security guys had actually collapsed in laughter. Randy was shaking with laughter; I could hardly keep a straight face. I wasn't sure whether he was real or not—we had a few of those, people who would come in and camp it up just to get on TV. "That was a joke, wasn't it?" I said. He shook his head. My mouth was literally hanging open. "In my opinion," I said, "you are the worst singer in the world." What shocked me was how shocked *he* was. This guy had just murdered Madonna's "Like a Virgin," and he was standing there amazed that I hadn't praised his vocal. I remember thinking that he was going to be famous—but for exactly the wrong reasons. This is what makes *American Idol* so compelling: the Keiths, who believe that they are somehow the second coming of Elvis Presley. I find it absolutely astonishing. He was so disillusioned, so genuine in his misunderstanding. I don't think we'll ever find another Keith. On second thought, I wouldn't bet on that.

Next stop: Nashville. I had never been to Nashville before, and I found the place quite odd. From the start, it was like stepping onto a film set, and while the people were fun, the place didn't seem quite real. The whole town revolves around country music and the music industry in general, so everywhere you go, you see people who look as if they have been sent from central casting. It was like a miniature version of Los Angeles, but also strangely intimate. What was most hysterical about Nashville was that no one who auditioned there was actually *from* there. They had come there to pursue their dream: They had driven six hours, eight hours, even ten hours. Still, the city generated more talent than most other places; as in Atlanta, many of the kids who showed up in Nashville had been trained as church singers, so they knew what they were doing.

The people I remember from Nashville include Rickey Smith, whom we all really liked as a person when we met him. He wasn't the best singer I've ever heard, but after we put him through, he clapped his hands together like a seal and started shouting, "Hercules, Hercules!" I found out later that the expression was from a scene in the Eddie Murphy movie *The Nutty Professor,* but at the time I hadn't a clue as to why he was doing that. We also met Corey Clark in Nashville, and Paula fell for him instantly; she thought he could be another Justin Guarini, though he had a twinkle in his eye and it was clear that he was a bit more of a bad boy than Justin. Kimberly Locke also auditioned for us in Nashville, and she was yet another example of how the second season differed from the first. Kimberly was talented but she looked like an overweight librarian. And the same thing, of course, went for Ruben Studdard, who also came out of Nashville. Ruben was a big guy, as we all know now, but unlike a lot of other big guys or big girls, he didn't see this as a problem. Sometimes, overweight people come into the room as if their weight will be held against them. Most come in with a huge chip on their shoulder and seem almost embarrassed to be there. But Ruben was one of those people whose personality walked in even before he did, and when he sang we didn't think of him as a fat guy; we just thought about what a great singer he was. He impressed us as a throwback to Luther Vandross or Barry White, one of those types of singers whom we haven't seen in a while. He was fantastic, and he was a contender from the start.

By the time we left Nashville, though we were only halfway through the auditions, I was feeling more confident about the talent in the second series. Frenchie and Ruben were superb; Clay was a dark horse; and we had plenty of the usual polished girl singers. All in all, an interesting battle was shaping up—image versus talent.

It's a good thing Nashville was so promising, because Miami was next. I have always loved Miami: It's a beautiful city, and we always get a few more days off when we're there to relax. But for the second straight year, the talent turned out to be incredibly disappointing. I don't really understand it. I expected Miami to produce some wonderful Latin-flavored talent, the next Gloria Estefan, perhaps, but over the two years of *American Idol,* Miami has turned up nothing. No one was any good at all. The only person I can remember from Miami was a guy named Edgar, who came in and sang an Enrique Iglesias song. When he sang, he looked like he was in pain, like he was being tortured, but in reality we were the ones being tortured. His audition ended up with him lying on the floor in theatrical agony. We told him that under no circumstances in a million years would he ever be going through to the next round, but he ran out of the audition room and told everybody he was going to Los Angeles. He was crazy.

We were put up in a hotel about ten miles away from South Beach, and Ryan and I decided to switch over to the Shore Club, which is right on the beach. That night Ryan and I hosted a dinner for the crew at the Delano—Randy was off with his wife and kids, and I don't know where Paula was—and as we were approaching the hotel, I suggested that we tell everyone that we were going to pay, so that they could order what they wanted, have a good time, and so forth. The second we got there, Ryan stood up and announced that *he* had decided that we should pay, a crafty move to ensure that he was the one the crew liked the best. Immensely pleased with himself, he smirked at me and sat down at the table like a horrible little prince. I could have killed him.

Dinner was excellent, though—a lot of fun, with a real sense of camaraderie. But there was a twist at the end. At one point earlier in the day, one of the young guys on the crew—we called him Don Johnson because he was from Miami, strutted around in a white suit, and thought he knew everything about the city—had tried to ingratiate himself with me and Ryan by offering to plan the entire evening. Over dinner that night I noticed that there were about six guys standing around near the table. I asked Don Johnson who they were. He said they were security. "We don't want security," I said.

"But I've arranged it," he whined.

"Well, how do we pay them?" I asked.

"You don't have to pay them," he said. "It's my treat."

The security guys stayed with us until about five in the morning, and then, as we were winding down the night, one of them asked me to get paid. It appeared that Don Johnson hadn't arranged for anything. Ryan and I weren't carrying cash, and they wouldn't take a credit card, so we ended up going from ATM to ATM, trying to collect enough money. Don Johnson had vanished, drunk somewhere, I think, and that was lucky for him, because I felt like strangling him. The next day he told me he was all set to organize another outing, but I stopped him short and told him how furious I was. He had not only left us holding the bill, but he had succeeded in embarrassing us—it was humiliating being followed around all night by this ridiculous security entourage. He left the show soon after that. Good. He was a bloody idiot.

That night we went to a club, where Ryan put the moves on a cute girl who worked for the show. As far as I was concerned, Ryan wasn't going to get a girl if I wasn't, and I didn't want to because I was dating someone. We went back to the hotel, the three of us, and I was already in bed when I overheard Ryan out on the terrace, feeding this woman the most ridiculous lines imaginable. I actually heard him say, "I wonder why the stars in Miami are so much brighter than the stars in L.A.," and "This may sound corny, but I believe destiny brought us here." Then he actually said, "Your eyes match the color of the ocean." That was it. I walked out onto the terrace, started talking about work, and then suggested that the three of us stay up and watch the sun rise. "You know," the girl said, "I think I've got to leave now." As far as I'm concerned, I did her a favor; she would have seriously regretted spending the night with Ryan.

After Miami came Austin. I loved Austin, partly because the city had so much energy—it was loud all the time, the streets were filled with people having a great time, and all in all it was more like what I thought Nashville would be like—and partly because Ryan got only a little room at the hotel while I got the presidential suite. That infuriated him and delighted me. Sadly, the energy of the city didn't translate to talent. Austin had more costumed entertainers than any other city except possibly Oz. We had everything turn up—people came dressed as Christmas trees, lizards, Harry Potter look-alike wizards, and one guy even auditioned as a banana. Well, not really, but he wore the worst yellow suit I have ever seen in my life. One beautiful girl walked in, and I prayed that she could sing. She couldn't: Her version of "Unchained Melody" was the slowest audition I have ever heard. If we had let her finish it would have literally taken hours. One ray of light was an attractive blonde named Kimberly Caldwell. She was extremely professional, and Randy in particular really liked her. She went through to the next round.

From Austin, we made our way back to Los Angeles. By that time, I was absolutely exhausted. The only bright spot was that Paula and I, after bickering on the road, were getting along again—we were back in our houses instead of in hotels, and I think that helped defuse the tension. I have to say this about Paula—she doesn't mess around. If she's unhappy she'll tell you. And in a strange way I like that, because you get it out in the open. I hate walking on eggshells around people.

The L.A. auditions were decent, and we pulled in a few more contestants who were good but not brilliant. We then saw a guy named J. D., who was related to John Adams, the American president. He was a good-looking boy with good manners, he sang well enough, and he had a kind of clean-cut charisma. From that first meeting, I thought that on paper, he was among the favorites. He was a nice-looking boy, so girls would adore him; and he was also a guy's guy, so boys would respect him. He had the full package not just as a singer but as an Idol. Then we met Josh Gracin, who from the start knew what his role was in the competition. He was the patriot, representing the Marines, and he literally marched into the audition room, saluted us, and stood at attention. His presence couldn't have been more perfectly tailored to the national climate at that time, and when he sang, he was good enough to impress us with his talent.

So at last, we had our pool. I thought Frenchie and Ruben were the front-runners in one sense, and J. D. and Josh in another sense. And Clay, of course, lurked in the back of everyone's mind as a truly bizarre talent to keep an eye on.

The Stars
Come Out

When it came time to narrow the field from the regional winners to the final group, I noticed that we had more determined and focused contestants than the first year. We also had more determined parents. In fact, I must have had propositions from three or four mothers, women who made it quite clear that while their son or daughter was onstage they might be available for a little something extra. I never let it get past a little flirting—when you are dealing with a competition like this, you have to steer absolutely clear of the contestants or their families. Oh, and I have a girlfriend.

We actually took over two hundred people back to Glendale, and our job was to find thirty-two finalists. It was around this time that the field of contestants began to follow its own internal dynamic, and I noticed right away that Ruben was often the center of attention. Whenever there was a group song, the other performers would stand in a ring around him. There was something instinctive about it, the same way that you could look at early 'N Sync performances and see that Justin Timberlake was the center, or look at early Supremes performances and see that Diana Ross was the center, even though neither of them was necessarily the strongest singer in their group. The X Factor affects the other performers just as it affects an audience, and people are often intuitively aware of a front-runner or a leader. At this point, Clay was keeping to himself; I think he sensed that his image wasn't going to work and that he had to make some changes before he tried to grab the spotlight. The other person who was very prominent at that point was Frenchie Davis. She was calm, quiet, and supremely confident, and every time she performed, it was obvious that she would be put through to the next round. I did an interview around that time in which I was asked who might win, and I mentioned Frenchie, Ruben, Clay (I called him "the kid with the big ears"), and Corey. Corey, at that point, was already a rebel—he went out partying one night, didn't learn his material, and gave a terrible performance the next day. That didn't surprise me so much, given that he was a twenty-two-year-old suddenly thrust into the spotlight, but I remember taking him aside and telling him to be careful.

There were also squabbles between the contestants, particularly the female contestants—most notably between Kimberly

I DON'T MEAN TO BE RUDE, BUT . . .
Sex Sells Only in the Records

Personally, I have had two instances where people tried to sell me artists with sex. More than ten years ago, I had a guy who brought a girl into my office. Her name was Maxine. He was her manager, and he looked like a secondhand car dealer and acted like one. She didn't say a word, just stood there in a long coat while he told me that she was going to be the next Madonna. When he put on her demo, it was awful, and I said so. He said, "I think we all know what it takes to be a star, and she's good at that—show him, Maxine." She then took off her coat to show that she was naked. I had to throw them both out of the office. Another time, in the wake of the Spice Girls, a manager brought in a new girl band; they ran into the office in their underwear and jumped in my lap and made it perfectly clear that they would sleep with me if I signed them. Neither of those artists got signed. In the higher echelons of the music industry, I think it happens much less than people think. Maybe some guy out at a club says they know the cousin of an agent, and a girl goes home with him because of it. But not in the real record business. Years ago, when record contracts were $50,000 maybe, but now a new artist costs two to three million to launch properly. That's an expensive screw.

Caldwell and Julia DeMato. In the small-group exercises, the contestants had to prepare a song and some choreography with three or four other performers, and Kimberly and Julia clearly didn't mix. In the parts that were shown on TV, Kimberly looked like the villain, but I'm not sure that was the case; I think Julia was already showing diva tendencies. Already, this bunch struck me as much more ambitious and competitive than the season-one contestants; if they were more diverse in terms of their talent, they were also more focused on their goal. The first time we did *American Idol,* no one really understood how it differed from any other talent show or variety show. Unless a contestant went online and researched the British version—and very few did—they didn't know what they were getting themselves into. The second-year crop knew everything. They had watched as Kelly Clarkson was delivered from obscurity into stardom; they knew the format of the show, the level of the competition, and the value of the prize. In the span of just one year, the naive amateurs had all disappeared and they had been replaced by hardened competitors. One or two were already very aware that personality would make a major difference this year.

Even so, the field of finalists was pretty easy to determine. Some singers had talent and others—most others—didn't. Any process like this is designed to nurture talent. If you're a good judge, you know that. And I am a very good judge. All the people we liked at this point weren't perfect by any stretch. They all had problems, either with their delivery or their song selection or their fashion sense or their confidence. You could argue that the only one of the thiry-two finalists who had no evident flaws was J. D. Adams, and ultimately he didn't last very long. We were looking for the people with the greatest potential, the singers and performers who could be molded and encouraged. Frenchie, Ruben, Clay—all of them had a talent, that was clear, and most important, they were unique in their own way. I was very excited about having a different kind of performer this year and very keen to see how the voting public would react.

Throughout the audition period, there was one singer who was, without question, the most groveling contestant I had ever met in my life. He was the ultimate brown-noser; he had this forced smile and was always complimenting us. We met him on the road in Nashville, and he was quite a good singer, but there was something about his personality that was difficult to trust. Sure enough, when Corey stayed out late, this other contestant was the one who snitched on him. That, for me, was unacceptable—you should never, ever sabotage a fellow contestant—and I decided that we should kick him out. The minute he was told that he wasn't going through, he showed his true colors: He heaped abuse on all of us, swore, nearly knocked Paula over, and even threatened legal action. My suspicions were correct.

The moment when we finally picked those thirty-two finalists was probably the only moment in the competition when I had the contestants' undivided attention. They were euphoric, and there was a sense of achievement rather than simple competitiveness. They were also quite receptive and eager for advice. I went in to talk to them with a representative from 19 Management. "Look," I said, "it's the chance of a lifetime. Ten of you will make it through to the final, and each of the ten of you will get national television exposure. You'll get put up in a mansion. You'll be driven around in limousines. Photographers will take your pictures. Everyone will want to shake your hand. But it's going to be hard work, and when I say that, I mean that. Because of that, I just want to tell you now that if you're not prepared to put in the hard work, you might as well get out of the competition." I also told them to enjoy the experience. I think they understood the lecture, at least some of them did. Many looked even more determined. By this time, we had heard all about the contestants' love for singing, and their innate need to entertain, but it was clear to me at that moment that they were beginning to focus on the prize. Show me a contestant who tells you that they're not on *American Idol* for the money, and I'll show you a liar.

The show was due to air in the middle of January, and as the date drew near, people kept telling us that we shouldn't expect the success of the first season. I said that I *did* expect the same success, and that, moreover, I thought we had a better show. Part of my thinking came from this year's contestants, which was a much more interesting mix, but part came from the fact that we were going to show more of the early auditions. I was sure that audiences would respond to that, because it showcased what's inherently funny about the industry—the egos, the delusions, the tantrums, and of course the singers who were horrendous but believed they were the second coming. People kind of shook their heads sadly when I raved about the new season, but I was right. The first episode drew something like twenty-nine million viewers, and for about a week my phone wouldn't stop ringing. At that point, the *American Idol* phenomenon was firmly in place. We were on magazine covers, on the evening news. The show was huge, and wherever we went, people knew our names.

Then I got a phone call from Nigel Lythgoe.

"Simon," he said, "we have a problem." Frenchie Davis, one of the odds-on favorites, had posed for an adult Web site some years before. Now her pictures had been discovered, and Nigel and Kenny thought she might have to be removed from the show.

I thought it was a tough call. As a record executive, I would keep her in. But if I was in Fox's shoes, protecting a billion-dollar brand, I didn't think I would risk offending family sponsors. There were subtler issues at play as well: At the auditions Frenchie had made it quite clear that she was trying to better her life, and I wondered if maybe we weren't sending the wrong message by kicking her off. To Fox's credit, they spent weeks agonizing over the decision. But in the end they decided that she would have to go. I felt disappointed for Frenchie, but in a way she had skipped to the end of the competition. Of that early group, she was hands down the most famous, the one contestant everyone had already heard about. She may have gotten more than she bargained for, but she withstood the controversy and ended up in New York City with a prime role in the musical *Rent*.

For the heats, we had divided the finalists into groups of eight, and they performed one after the other. The first group was just awful. Because they all knew about the first season, and because this critical step had been on their minds since the earliest auditions, they had rehearsed their music to death. It looked like they had spent hours and hours in front of the mirror, trying to perfect what they were doing, and it was dull and lifeless. To me, it looked as if they were just trying to get through the ordeal rather than win the competition. J. D. Adams, one of my early picks, was absolutely terrible. I was sorry we had put him through; it just goes to show that a pretty face isn't everything. The only thing that made it amusing was the fact that one of the kids, Patrick Fortson, came out looking like a penguin. Literally. He sang well enough, and all the judges agreed on that, but Randy and I simply could not let his outfit pass without comment. It was the worst suit I've ever seen in my life. Paula said she liked it (what a surprise), but I had to say something. "If you won the competition," I said, "and we put out a CD with you wearing that outfit, it wouldn't sell a single copy." That brought his very stylishly dressed dad out to complain. I said to both of them that if Patrick had dressed like his dad, he might have had a chance. That incident probably got more attention in the media than any of the singers. The two that made it through that week were Julia DeMato and Charles Grigsby. At the time, I couldn't even remember Charles, but apparently we'd seen him in Detroit and he was just okay. He was a nonfactor in every sense of the word, a nice enough kid who worked in a supermarket, liked to sing, and had the charisma of a goldfish—a very understated goldfish. Kimberly Caldwell, Julia's former nemesis, just missed the cut. There was no question that the previous film clip had hurt her. All in all it was unremarkable, and in my mind there wasn't an American Idol, or anyone close, in the bunch. Not everyone agreed: Julia DeMato went on a radio station the next day and announced that my opinion no longer mattered, because she had made it through on her own merit. I thought, we'll see.

The second group were in a different league, with Ruben, Clay, and Kimberly Locke. Ruben was phenomenal: confident, enthusiastic, wonderful. Kimberly was probably the best singer in the competition, technically, but she didn't seem to have a personality, which is what I said to her after that first performance. She then attacked me. "I used to think you were sexy," she said, "but you suck." Randy and Paula delighted in this; they gave each other high fives, and Kimberly left the stage grinning. This was fine with me—I didn't mind the contestants arguing back—but the fact remained that she lacked star quality. She could be a session singer, and a very good one, and make quite a comfortable living. But I didn't look at her and think, "superstar." Clay, on the other hand, was a revelation. He had done some kind of makeover, and it was like he was a different person—his glasses were gone and his hair was lighter. It was a bold effort, but he didn't quite make it. He fell just short in the vote and was left behind. He was totally devastated after the results came through.

The third group was just as disappointing as the first, and turned out to be the source of some controversy. A contestant named Vanessa Oliveras, a fiery little Spanish girl, came on, and she had put on a bit of weight since we last saw her. Vanessa, to me, was like a cross between Bette Midler and Cyndi Lauper, though not as good as either. She was all about her bubbly personality rather than her singing ability, although she was an extremely nice girl. She never took herself seriously, and she was one of those people who was exactly the same off camera as she was on camera. I liked her performance, but told her I thought she could stand to lose a few pounds. Talk about lighting a powder keg. Suddenly, we were being called out in the media for promoting unhealthy body image and even told that we might have thinness-challenged people picketing the show. One of the people who took sides against me on that issue, surprise surprise, was Paula. She went on *Entertainment Tonight* and said that certain people in the media were encouraging weight disorders. I don't know if she named me by name, but just after her comments, they rolled the clip of me talking to Vanessa. I thought Paula was out of order. Even my best defense got me in trouble. I had never said anything about weight loss to Ruben or Frenchie, but in some people's minds, that made me a hypocrite. My point was this: There was no reason to tell Ruben to drop a few pounds—it would have taken months. That was who he was. But Vanessa was just a girl who got a bit out of shape, and I felt that I was justified in telling her that. Truth be told, if Ruben did come to me and ask for my advice, I would recommend weight loss to him for health reasons. Anyway, Vanessa got through, as did Rickey Smith. But neither of them had a cat in hell's chance of winning the competition.

Show four added Corey Clark and Joshua Gracin to the mix. At that point, Josh was getting a bit of pressure from certain reporters, who wanted to know why he was participating in a singing competition when there was a war brewing with Iraq. During the show, I deliberately singled him out. "Josh," I said, "if we went to war and your unit was called into duty, what would you do with regard to your role in this competition?"

He looked straight at me and said, "Simon, I'm a Marine." I wanted him to get through—I thought he was a nice kid—but I also wanted to give him a chance to be clear about his patriotism. See, I am a nice person sometimes.

Last but not least was the wild-card show, which brought back contestants who had been eliminated and gave them another chance. In theory it was a wonderful thing. In practice it was disastrous. Hardly any of the people we brought back to compete for the remaining finalist spots shone. No one, that is, except for Clay. He performed Elton John's "Don't Let the Sun Go Down on Me," and he was superb, in a totally different league than the others. Kimberly Caldwell, who had been close the first time around, had an off night with Carole King's "I Feel the Earth Move," but she was still worlds better than the rest. So Kimberly and Clay were a given. The only problem was that we still had to find two more: Fox wanted twelve finalists instead of ten, to extend the competition. Paula really liked a girl named Trenyce, who sang a good version of Al Green's "Let's Stay Together," and put her through. Randy picked Kimberly Caldwell; he was always a big fan. I knew America would pick Clay, so I picked Carmen Rasmusen, a young girl from Utah who had a decent voice and a great personality, and who brought something I felt we were missing at this stage of the competition. In fact, she was the youngest contestant to be moved to the next round; she was only seventeen years old at the time. But what I saw in her was the fact that she was commercial, simple as that. I thought that she could one day have a real recording career, and that's what the show is about. We now had our twelve finalists, and we were ready for the homestretch.

At around that time, there was a big question-and-answer session organized by the Television Academy. Various members of the press and the academy interviewed both the on-air talent and the contestants. It was my first opportunity to see the whole dirty dozen in one place. My initial impulse had been right; it was a more interesting, diverse, and exciting group than the first year, and I was suddenly very optimistic. We had our divas, of course—Trenyce and Kimberly Caldwell and Julia DeMato—but we also had types of singers that we hadn't seen before. As the contestants answered questions and bantered with the press, what struck me was that there was one who was head and shoulders above everyone else: Clay. He was witty and self-effacing. He had researched and prepared. And, as the number of signs and banners at the session showed, he already had a following.

SHOOTING AT STARS
Simon Takes Aim at the Famous

I am always being asked, "What would you say to today's music superstars if they showed up at an *American Idol* audition?" Hmm. Now that would be interesting.

Bob Dylan: "Too ugly, too boring, too whiny, and too serious."

Mariah Carey: "Great voice; lose the attitude."

Whitney Houston: "Yes, but drop the husband."

Michael Jackson: "NEXT!"

Jon Bon Jovi: "No. Don't like your hair."

J.Lo: "No."

Elton John: "Yes, if you lose a few pounds."

'N Sync: "No, no, no, no, and the one with the curly hair—yes."

Ruben, too, was very popular, and Kimberly Locke had come a long way since her audition. Afterward, there were loads of fans clustered at the exits, and the contestants went to sign autographs. I remember watching Ruben, who suddenly had access to cute girls (and was beaming like a Cheshire cat); watching Clay, who showed that he absolutely loved fame; and watching Kimberly Locke, who was basking in her own transformation. Interestingly, there were three or four girls who were already beginning to act like divas. This is the point where we started to see the true personalities of our finalists, and they weren't all pretty.

Back in
the Spotlight

The second season's first live show was the first time that Ryan Seacrest had hosted *American Idol* on his own: no Brian Dunkleman to rain on his parade. If I could have bottled his happiness and sold it, I would be a billionaire rather than just a millionaire. He could hardly contain himself. The first night of the live shows, we all got together beforehand—well, eventually we all did, after all the primping and preening. Paula has her own hair and makeup people, and she spends about three hours getting ready. Randy and I take about five minutes each. Ryan takes three and a half hours. And then he has his hair done. In my dressing room, at some point, Randy and Ryan and I ended up gossiping about the new season. Randy was the fount of all gossip—he seemed to know everything. But we also talked to the makeup and hair people. It gave us an insight into the kids' behavior. The makeup people would tell us who was especially nice and who was consistently a pain in the ass. Trenyce, for example, wasn't well liked by the makeup and hair people, and we heard about that on a regular basis. That makeup period was also the only time we could actually be free of the contestants, thanks to a rule we had passed that barred them from our backstage area. It was necessary, because during the first season lots of contestants would come backstage and try to ingratiate themselves with the judges before a live show. The atmosphere in rehearsals that day had been very tense; the kids were dead serious about the competition, and they were all terrified of being the first one cut.

My pleasure in seeing the second live season finally get under way was tempered by the fact that the executive producers and Fox, at long last, had added a fourth judge, just as they had always threatened to do. In fact, they had added a series of them: We were now supposed to welcome a different celebrity on each show to help us comment on the contestants (hooray!). I wasn't in favor of this idea at all. I understood why the network was doing it, but I felt it undermined our credibility and threw off our chemistry. It also, frankly, cut into our time. Because I'm not shy, I let my feelings be known in the press, and after that I ended up having a heated argument with one of the executive producers. "If you think it's such a good idea," I said, "why don't you bring in a celebrity executive producer next week?" He didn't see the humor in it.

BEHIND THE SCENES
Things You Never Knew About the Second Season

★ Clay always bought his shoes one size too big, because he hates having his toes touch the end.

★ Julia DeMato's mother bought all of Julia's initial clothes at the casino store with her winning chips.

★ When Kimberly Caldwell was shopping in Diesel one day, there were no available changing rooms, so she stripped stark naked outside the changing area and the *American Idol* stylists had to frantically find things to cover her.

★ Trenyce was packed and ready to leave the show for four weeks before she was actually voted off.

★ Carmen was never allowed to show her shoulders, midriff or anything above the knee, as requested by the priest at her church.

The first person we judged with was Lamont Dozier, the legendary Motown songwriter who, with his partners Brian and Eddie Holland, was responsible for countless hits recorded by Martha and the Vandellas ("Heat Wave"), Marvin Gaye ("Can I Get a Witness"), The Four Tops ("Standing in the Shadows of Love"), and especially the Supremes (Holland-Dozier-Holland wrote ten Top-10 hits for the group, including "Baby Love," "Stop! In the Name of Love," and "You Keep Me Hanging On"). That night, the kids were all singing Motown hits. The show was fairly uneventful, with the exception of Clay's ongoing transformation. That week, he had a new hairstyle and he had fixed his teeth. It was as if he were serving notice to the rest of the contestants—and the viewers—that he was determined to go all the way. For me, it didn't quite work, because in those early live shows he was beginning to perform like some ghastly Las Vegas cabaret act—horrible dance moves, embarrassing winks to the camera. All the singers were nervous, and Vanessa, who wasn't by any means the worst, got voted off. She was very philosophical after the show; she told me that she knew she would never win, and was just grateful for the opportunity. Weeks later she posed naked for some pictures—not a pretty sight.

The second week the famous soul singer Gladys Knight—best known for her hit "Midnight Train to Georgia" and her backup group the Pips—came on, and I have to say she was very good. She was more animated than Lamont Dozier, and had thought through her role very carefully. She's the one, in fact, who coined Ruben's nickname: After he sang "A Whole New World," she called him a "velvet teddy bear." The name stuck—to this day, it's how Ruben is known, and they have even started manufacturing velvet teddy bears to sell to his fans. Charles Grigsby left, and that was no surprise at all. He had barely been there to start with. He was very upset after being voted off; he had been working in a supermarket before the show and had now tasted stardom. I think the competition is especially tough on kids like Charles, who see *American Idol* as an escape. The sad reality is that I can see Charles back in the supermarket within two years.

The week after that, our celebrity judge was Olivia Newton-John. She was very flirtatious, with a glint in her eye. In fact, she asked me to dinner after the show, which put to rest my notion that she was some kind of good girl. But I couldn't go. As a judge, she was less interesting—she didn't want to offend anyone, and it showed. That night, the theme was country music. I hate country music. I mean, now and again I'll hear something I like, but I loathe the vast majority of it. Most of the songs seem to be about missing a dog. I thought it was bizarre that I was being asked to judge country performances. I shouldn't even have turned up that day. Some of the performances were very good—Ruben, in particular, turned in a terrific version of the rock song "Sweet Home Alabama"—but my worst suspicions were confirmed when Josh Gracin came out and sang a Garth Brooks song wearing an enormous Stetson. Something about him sounded different. No: Everything about him sounded different. His voice was deeper, and he even had an accent. "Josh," I said, "what on earth has happened to your voice?"

"Well, I love country music," he said.

"That's news to me," I said. "You never mentioned it before. And now you seem to have a completely different voice than you did last week."

"Now I'm a country singer," he said.

"Next week's a different theme," I said. "Are you going to change your voice again?"

"No," he said. "I'll still sing country."

"So you'll be a country singer singing disco? Fine." We went back and forth for a little while, and he got more and more stubborn, petulant even, which I found irritating. It wasn't so much that I hated his performance, though I did hate it. I just felt that it was a massive error on his part both creatively and strategically. Here we were, fairly late in the competition, and he was introducing a whole new Josh Gracin, which threw everything off. He had proved that he could mimic Garth Brooks, but we weren't looking for a mimic. The best singers on that show, whether Ruben or Clay or Kimberly, had their own style, and it was sometimes so strong that they had to fight to vary their sound. What Josh was doing was very risky. I also noticed that he was taking my criticism less well as the competition went along. It may have had something to do with his wife; she intensely wanted him to win. She was always backstage, and during the competition she rarely spoke to me. Josh seemed to be under a tremendous amount of pressure, and I think it harmed his judgment. As the competition went on, he showed me more and more that he had some growing up to do.

Ultimately, Josh survived that week though—it was Julia DeMato who didn't make it, after a mediocre performance of Faith Hill's "Breathe" in which she really struggled. She turned off the voters, and they turned on her and eliminated her. I used to call Julia the Joan Collins of *American Idol*, because she had that same air that Joan Collins did when she was the villain in *Dynasty*. I meant it in a good way. She was the girl all the other girls loved to hate—she had a great body, and while she was just an attractive girl when we first saw her, she had transformed herself as the series moved along, coloring her hair, wearing sexier clothing, until she ended up as a sexy little minx. If only she had transformed her dancing, which was abysmal; she looked as if she was in pain out there on the stage. I liked Julia's parents very much—her dad could have been in *The Sopranos* or the Rat Pack; he had a kind of natural cool and swagger that was very entertaining. Personally, Julia was one of the few contestants whom I would have liked to have seen socially, because she made me laugh and actually didn't take herself too seriously. For some reason, though, the viewing public never warmed to her. I have a hunch they found her intimidating.

Julia's departure also furnished a perfect example of one of the unspoken rules of *American Idol:* the crying rule. It's easy to understand. When someone is eliminated, someone else has to cry. Why? Because it's so sad to watch your "close friend's" career nipped in the bud. Yeah, right! Never mind that the people who are eliminated usually deserve it, and that the remaining contestants are ecstatic that their competition has taken a tumble. And if one person cries, then everybody has to cry. Again, why? Because no one wants to be singled out for being heartless. Remember, the competition is televised, and the contestants are aware of the cameras at all times. If one of the cameramen happens to swing a lens toward you and you're not crying, you look heartless, and that won't get you far with viewers—before long, you'll be the one leaving while other people are pretending to cry. So they all do it. They weep. They sob. They're heartbroken. That night, Julia got thrown off, and everyone was so grief-stricken that you would have thought she was being sent off to the gallows to be hanged. Kimberly Caldwell, who had never really gotten along with her, cried so much that her mascara ran. She was standing onstage looking like the Lone Ranger, bawling her eyes out over the departure of the girl who had been her rival, and not always a friendly rival, since day one.

The next week the theme was disco and our celebrity judge was one of the kings of seventies funk and soul, Verdine White, who played bass for Earth, Wind and Fire. Verdine was indisputably a musical hero for those of us old enough to remember Earth, Wind and Fire—Randy, who was a bassist before he was an A&R executive, was especially impressed—but he was also one of the strangest people I have ever met. He was extremely nice, but his preshow ritual took him at least five hours, and included at least three bottles of aftershave. And his clothes were like a costume: skintight leather pants and a white frilly shirt that looked like he'd gotten them out of a time machine.

That week, for some reason, no one was any good. Rickey Smith walked out in a ridiculous afro wig that didn't work at all. Josh's performance of Kool and the Gang's "Celebration" was another low point; he had a cold, he said, and he sounded abominable. It was painful to hear, and I explained to him that if he had sung that badly when he had first auditioned, he never would have gotten within a mile of the stage. It was actually one of the worst performances of the series. Despite the fact that a disco show should have been great fun, no one had any fun at all. Even Ryan got very annoyed with me that night; after Kimberly Locke sang, "It's Raining Men," I told her she had just sung Ryan's favorite song. He wasn't amused. The following night on the results show he retaliated with some other gay comment. The next thing I knew, we were being criticized for being homophobic. That, of course, is ridiculous, especially since at the same time I was being accused of being gay. Now and again, you'd see it in newspapers or hear it from comedians. They would say, "Simon's single, and he wears those tight T-shirts, and there's something about him that I can't quite put my finger on."

I think this is the proper time for me to come out and admit the truth, which is that I'm straight. Maybe it's true that I don't like the traditional macho things. I don't play rugby. I don't drink beer. I don't hang out in pubs. I take an interest in what I wear. And I'm forty-three years old and single. But if I were gay, I would happily admit it—I'm in an industry where it's not a problem, and if I was, who would care? I have been dating my current girlfriend, Terri, for about a year now—she was with me through most of the second season of *American Idol*. I met her about ten years ago, through a friend of mine I used to date, a girl called Laura, and Terri was a model at the time. We saw each other on and off through the years, but at that point nothing had ever happened between us. Years later, Terri came to stay with me for a week in Los Angeles and ended up staying for a year! We get on really well. One of the main reasons is that we can both laugh at most things, including ourselves. In this business that's important.

As for the fact that I'm not married, well, I have my own reasons. I have so many friends who are married and miserable, and I'm single and happy. To me, marriages seem like work. After a certain amount of time in any relationship, the buzz goes away, and then it's time to move on. I live in mortal terror of being half of one of those ghastly silent couples you see in restaurants. They're sitting there across from one another, staring at each other, and saying absolutely nothing. They resent each other to no end, because they're stuck, either because of children or money or respect for the vows they made. Working in the entertainment business for this long, I have come to have a slightly different view of contracts. I think very carefully before I sign a contract with an artist, and that's for only a few years. So I am cynical about entering into a contract with a girl that lasts a lifetime. I love kids, but I think I'm probably too old to start a family now. I wouldn't rule it out entirely, but I'd hate to be the old dad who can't relate to them when they go off to college.

At any rate, the rumors were flying fast and furious, and to make matters even more ridiculous, there was a second set of rumors that suggested that I was having an affair with Paula, and that our arguments were just a way of covering up our secret backstage passion. The gay jokes that night, I'm sure, only confused people further. Good.

While the performances on the disco show were shockingly

I DON'T MEAN TO BE RUDE, BUT . . .
Only Idiots Hate Disco

I always think that whenever you compare the music of the era you grew up in to the music of today you sound like a boring old fart. But I genuinely believe that the disco era was one of the best times for pop music—ever. To me it epitomizes everything that is good about music: having fun, dancing, glamour, excess, and girls. It was camp but sexy, and some of the best dance records of all time came out of that movement, from Chic's "Good Times" and "Le Freak" to Donna Summer's classic "I Feel Love." The lyrics were mostly about having a good time, and in that pre-AIDS culture, sex appeal was extremely important. Disco exploded worldwide when the BeeGees brought the movement to the silver screen with the soundtrack to *Saturday Night Fever.* After that—shock, horror—boys started dancing in clubs.

For three years, from 1977 to 1980, disco ruled the world. Even artists like Rod Stewart got in on the act by making disco singles. Rod had his biggest hit ever with the disco version of "Do Ya Think I'm Sexy." Today, twenty-five years later, the songs still sound amazing, and I wonder—if *American Idol* is on thirty years from now, will we devote a week to the Wu Tang Clan?

bad, we also had a bit of drama when Corey Clark was disqualified for being under criminal investigation. The only reason we hadn't found out before was that the police had spelled his name wrong in the original complaint. When it came to light, we had to ask him to leave. I felt sorry to see him go. Corey was one of the few guys who would hang out after the show; he had a good sense of humor, and I never felt that he was putting on an act. I think some of the girls were sorry to see him go as well, because apparently he'd had a threesome with two of them. (I can't say for certain who it was—I obviously wasn't there—but according to speculation, the two girls were Kimberly Caldwell and Trenyce.) Because Corey was kicked off for legal reasons, we didn't remove any of the contestants. They got a free pass, and some of them were relieved, as they should have been—many managed to squeak by with incredibly bad performances. That night, on the live show, I said, "At least two of you are lucky to still be in this competition." Josh ran up to me after the show and said, "You were talking about me, weren't you?" I told him to draw his own conclusions.

On the fifth show, the theme was *Billboard* number-one hits, and the judge was my favorite celebrity judge, Lionel Richie. He had a fantastic sense of humor, was as smart as a whip, and was as musically astute as anyone I had ever met. It was great fun to work with him. One of the kids—Rickey, I think, who would end up being voted off that night—sang one of Lionel's songs, and afterward Lionel praised him by saying that he had sung it almost as well as the original. As soon as he finished, I said, "With all the greatest respect, Lionel, I never particularly liked your original." He looked over at me, and it took him about a millionth of a second to realize that I was joking. But the audience thought it was real, and he played along with it. And for weeks afterward, he continued to play along when he appeared on talk shows, even though when I met him at events and so forth, we joked about it. Soon the Lionel Richie insult took on a life its own. Clive Davis, who runs RCA Records in America and is one of the true moguls of the record business, called me one day and complained about my treatment of Lionel. I tried to explain it to him, but Clive is very old-fashioned about respect and he wasn't very happy about it.

That same night, two contestants turned away some kids after the show who were looking for autographs. This, to me, was a cardinal sin—you never treat your fans poorly, and especially not at the beginning of your career, when the demands are relatively light and you absolutely depend on each and every supporter to maintain your fame. I spoke to them privately the next day. I said, "I have heard it confirmed from three people that you refused to sign autographs—worse, that you rolled up the windows on the car and drove off while the kids were standing there."

They sort of avoided my gaze and said they were tired.

This type of behavior really pisses me off. I told them, "If you do it again, I'm going to make your behavior known to all of America, and I'm sure that the public won't appreciate it very much."

They didn't do it again as far as I know, and true to my word, I won't reveal their names.

In the middle of the series, war broke out. The producers and the Fox executives were put in a very difficult situation, because

we had a number-one show in America at a time when all entertainment suddenly seemed frivolous. A Fox executive called me
to say that they weren't going to pull the show, but that they
needed us to be slightly more stately, to tone down the comedy.
A woman named Susan, who worked for Freemantle, came up
with the brilliant idea of having the kids sing Lee Greenwood's
country song "I'm Proud to Be an American" on the results
show. To say that the song got a reaction was an understatement.
It was an incredible moment. The kids totally got into the song
and were visibly moved by the lyrics, the audience was spell-
bound, and even a usually cynical judge like myself was touched.
The phones were ringing off the hook. It was so powerful that
Mike Darnell insisted upon another performance of the song.
Prior to that, we had planned on releasing a single with the cast
singing Burt Bacharach's "What the World Needs Now Is Love."
We'd recorded the song already and it turned out very well, but
after the tremendous response to the war show, we decided to
release both singles. It was a perfect example of how a show like
ours could work for the public good—and even touch on the
current political climate—without being disrespectful.

The show after that was devoted to the songs of Billy Joel. He
couldn't make it, so Smokey Robinson filled in as a celebrity
guest judge. He was a nice guy, Smokey, although he does look
like something out of a zombie movie with those strange gray
eyes. As much as it pains me to say it, that show with Smokey
was the first time that I realized that Paula Abdul was a bloody

good judge. It had taken me all of one year and most of the next, but I finally saw how much she meant to the show and how sincere she was about singing and performing. I don't always agree with her, obviously, and I don't agree with consistently supporting the underdog at times and giving them false hope, but she had become, over time, an integral part of the show. Paula is incredibly entertaining to watch. That show was also the first time that I realized that Kimberly Locke might actually win. She had toned down her fashion sense and her hair—at times it had been just insane, as if she had been struck by lightning—and she just latched on to her song, which was "New York State of Mind," and boy did she sing it well.

At this point, I was beginning to feel that Ruben and Clay were in a bit of a rut. Ruben did a Barry White–style cover of "Just the Way You Are," and I criticized him for the first time. I told him he was playing it safe and becoming one-dimensional as a result. There was a gasp from the audience, and Ruben himself visibly jerked back as if he were stung. I'm sure the other contestants loved it, because we had been so sycophantic to him by that point that I had almost run out of compliments. This was also the week where Josh challenged me to a push-up competition and lost. They didn't show it all on television, but let the record show that the twenty-two-year-old Marine lost to the forty-three-year-old record producer.

After the show, Ruben said, "Can I have a word with you, Simon?"

"Certainly," I said. I didn't know what to expect.

We went off to the side, and he took a deep breath. "You know," he said, "that was the best advice anyone has ever given me. You're absolutely right. I was falling into a trap here, and I'll think about what you said." I was impressed that Ruben had the maturity to respond this way.

The next night, Kimberly Caldwell was voted off. I wasn't bothered. It was clear from the first time we met her that she was one of those people who had wanted to be a star from the time she was a little girl. Every picture we saw of her growing up, she was always putting on a show. You could imagine her parents having to suffer through those ghastly renditions from the miniature Kimberly, encouraging her because they loved her while secretly wishing she would stop. From my perspective, her problem was that she had done it for too long. She had a good commercial singing voice, but there was just too much cabaret in her—too much slickness—to make her credible. She didn't like the criticism I threw at her; in fact, she took it quite personally. But that was that. She was gone. But in the end, her elimination was trivial. The real story of the night was Ruben. There was now a different energy emanating from the group; he wasn't perceived as invincible anymore.

The following week, my close friend Diane Warren came on to be our guest judge. Diane is one of the most successful songwriters of all time; she's written hits for Celine Dion, LeAnn Rimes, Toni Braxton, Whitney Houston, and others. Diane is also one of the weirdest people I've ever met in my life. She's about forty-five years old, single, worth hundreds of millions of

I DON'T MEAN TO BE RUDE, BUT . . .
Even a Shower Cap Is Better Than a Suit

The great thing about Ruben was that he was such a happy guy. He's a big guy, but he's totally comfortable in his own skin. Ironically, when the show started to style him, when he was put in suits in the latter stages of the competition, I thought he lost his appeal slightly. I loved Ruben when he dressed himself and he had his baseball cap and his 205 T-shirt and his baggy jeans. I wouldn't trust any stylists in the world to tell me what a twenty-one- or twenty-two-year-old kid should be wearing who wants to get into pop music now unless they were twenty-one or twenty-two themselves. In other words, I wouldn't have had a clue how to dress Eminem if he'd come to me, even though I've been doing this job for so many years. He has his own sense of style, and he's worn some of the weirdest things on earth. The people in his videos have got shower caps on their heads; I mean the whole thing is ludicrous, but it sort of works. But if I had turned around to an artist ten years ago and said "I think it's cool to put a shower cap on your head," they would have laughed at me. Sometimes it pays to forgo convention and stick with your own instincts.

dollars, and is easily the most insecure and superstitious person in the world. In Los Angeles, right in the middle of her impeccable, modern publishing-company offices, there's a room that can only be described as hell on earth. It's the room where she wrote her first hit almost two decades ago, and she hasn't cleaned or dusted that room in all the time since. The curtains have rotted. The furniture is in pieces. Everything is covered in layers of dust, including an antiquated keyboard. When first Diane brought me into this room, I felt like I wanted to run. "I can't spend another second in here," I said. "Why are you working in this room?" The way she explained it, it was superstition: She was worried that if she changed rooms—or, for that matter, changed any-thing about the room itself—she would never have another hit. Of course, I told her she was crazy. But it wasn't until later that I got a chance to prove it to her. On the first *American Idol*, I had asked her to write a bunch of songs for Kelly Clarkson's album, but I didn't like any of them in the end. Some weeks later, I went to a party at her house in Malibu with Randy and his wife, Erica, and at two in the morning we were all sitting around drunk when Erica asked Diane to play a song she had heard her play years before called "Some Kind of Miracle." Diane played it on her grand piano in this incredible setting and our jaws just dropped—it ended up on Kelly's album. Diane won't admit it, but I think that experience partially cured her of her addiction to that dreadful room.

Diane's week was also the last week for Carmen Rasmusen. Carmen had been struggling to keep up for a few weeks, and her performances were fairly badly frayed by that point. Still, I was sorry to see her go; she was my pick from the wild-card show, and even though she was the longest of long shots, she was one of the few contestants who showed off her maturity throughout the competition. She didn't alienate anyone and didn't act the star even once. On the last show, she was true to form; she thanked everyone, and left with her dignity. Her parents thanked me for my support. I think in a weird way she was glad to go. I think she knew she could never win, but had enjoyed the experience enormously.

The next week, Neil Sedaka joined us, and well, there is only one Neil Sedaka. He spent about an hour anxiously preparing, jotting down notes during the rehearsals, and he came up with some of the most hilarious phrases I have ever heard, including the infamous "ear-delicious." That was Clay's night to shine: He sang a version of "Solitaire," which had been a hit for the Carpenters, that was absolutely breathtaking. It was one of the highlights of the whole series. He had the audience in the palm of his hand. "I think he's going to win," I whispered to Paula, and she agreed.

Then Trenyce came on, and she had overdone herself so much, with caked-on makeup, ridiculous high heels, and a completely ghastly dress that she looked like a Tina Turner drag act. I told her so, and she wasn't amused. Randy, in fact, called me out on it afterward. "Simon," he said. "You have gone too far." Randy didn't need to say much more than this; he spoke with his actions, which in this case included a day of silent treatment.

Justin Guarini was a guest on the results show the following night, when Ruben somehow fell into the bottom two and teetered on the brink of elimination. We were all shocked by this development, though in the back of my mind I thought that maybe his coasting had caught up with him. I didn't want him to be eliminated, of course—I had flashbacks to Tamyra's early departure the year before. Or rather, I had been having flashbacks all along, and I had done my best not to even fantasize about a Ruben-Clay final, lest I jeopardize it like I had jeopardized the Kelly-Tamyra final the first year. Luckily, Ruben made it through, and Trenyce was the one who was cut. I wasn't surprised. I never really warmed to her. If in the future we invent robots to sing, they should be modeled on Trenyce. She worked very hard at her image, too hard—she was the girl who was the most unpopular with the wardrobe and makeup people. There was a big round of applause in the makeup room when she got kicked off.

Robin Gibb closed out the run of celebrity judges the following week, when the four remaining contestants all sang BeeGees songs. That was my favorite week musically, although it started off on an embarrassing note. Some weekly magazine had run a huge feature about how much I hated the idea of the celebrity judges, which was true, and it seemed to put Robin off a bit, although I had nothing against him personally. In fact, I felt bad for him—his brother Maurice had just died. The songs, of course, were absolutely sensational; the BeeGees have produced so much great work, from their early pop songs through to their disco classics. Josh Gracin, in particular, sang brilliantly. Even though he had picked the same song, "To Love Somebody," as Clay, he held his own. Josh was eliminated; he didn't have the

I DON'T MEAN TO BE RUDE, BUT . . .
Maybe Clay's Makeover Should Have Been Reversed

Clay Aiken was the best example of somebody who used *American Idol* as the most gigantic makeover of all time. He changed his hair, his glasses, his teeth, his clothes. But in a strange way, I think he may have gone too far, at least for the purposes of the competition. Remember, Clay's appeal was the fact that he was the nerd with the great voice—i.e., the underdog. I believe that if Clay had walked into that audition room dressed and looking like he was on the night of the *American Idol* final, we wouldn't have put him through. It would have seemed odd and very theatrical. His appeal and his charm was the fact that he was an individual, and I remembered Clay way above all of the Britney clones, the Christina clones, the Justin Timberlake clones we had. The public, remember, likes individuality.

consistency to keep up with the others. But he had saved the best for last, and he went out with his dignity intact. The low point of the night—of the whole season, in fact, and maybe the low point in the history of filmed musical performances—was Clay's second appearance. He sang "Grease" wearing a red leather jacket, and he had an unbelievably awful dance routine to go along with it. Everything about it was horrible. And everything he'd accomplished the week before with Neil Sedaka's "Solitaire," which was stylish and sophisticated, was thrown away with just one performance. I still believe that it may have cost him the overall competition, because that performance was so terrible that it was hard to get past it in your mind.

After the Robin Gibb show, it was back to just the three of us—me, Randy, and Paula—but with a twist this time: Some of the songs would be selected by the judges. At this point, there were only three contestants left, and everyone thought Kimberly Locke was headed out the door.

But on the night of the semifinals, she walked onstage with a very determined look on her face; it said, "I know you're going to vote me off, but I'm going to prove to you how good I am." She sang "Band of Gold," "Anyone Who Had a Heart," and "Inseparable." In fact, she outsang Ruben by a wide margin; he sang "Smile," "Signed, Sealed, Delivered," and "If Ever I'm in Your Arms Again," and with the exception of "Smile," he sounded ragged, tired. Clay had the most eclectic selection, and he wasn't on form either: His rendition of Don McLean's "Vincent" was dreary, and he even forgot some of the words, and while he rescued himself somewhat with a superb "Mack the Knife" and a decent "Unchained Melody," I thought he could have done far better. On the basis of those performances alone, Kimberly deserved to be passed through to the final, but I hoped she wouldn't be. For starters, the competition wasn't dependent only on that night, but on week after week of performing in front of a national audience. Also, there was the fact that while I loved her performance, I desperately wanted a Ruben-Clay final. Thankfully, the audience agreed with me, forgave Ruben for a subpar night, and put Ruben and Clay through. Kimberly was quite cold with me afterward, for some reason. It wasn't shocking—she had always been much friendlier with Randy and Paula. She gave me a hug, but it was a weak hug, as if I were somewhat responsible for the way things turned out, rather than her. That's the thing about the show—no matter what the contestants think, and no matter how much they resent our opinions, it's ultimately the viewers who decide the outcome.

The Final

The night of the finale every radio station and newspaper wanted to do interviews with the judges and the contestants. I must have done over one hundred fifty interviews, and it was a boiling hot day in May. When I finally made it to the Universal Amphitheater, I discovered that Ryan had been given the biggest dressing room I have ever seen in my life, whereas I had been given the smallest. After a season of competition, he had the last laugh—in this regard.

I went down the hall to talk to Clay and Ruben, and both of them were extremely nervous. Ruben wasn't himself. He was sweating, he looked agitated, and for the first time he looked scared. Clay was only slightly less anxious. I wished them both luck; I told them that it had been a pleasure working with the two of them, and that they should enjoy the fact that they were performing in front of almost forty million people. I don't think they heard a word I said.

Both contestants had to sing three songs that night, and the first two performances from each were fairly disappointing. I knew, the audience knew, and both Ruben and Clay knew that so far, their performances were less than stellar. This was the climax to everything we had worked for—the final of *American Idol.* Where was the drama? Where was the wow factor? Now we were down to the third and final songs, and Ruben was to go first. The song he had chosen was a song called "Flying Without Wings," which had been a number-one hit for Westlife three years before.

Ruben walked out on the stage. I could see him steadying himself, aware that this was the last song he would sing in the competition. The audience was unusually quiet—they sensed that he could win or lose everything with this performance.

He started singing, and this was the Ruben we loved. You could see him lifting himself up throughout the song, and when the gospel choir joined him at the end it was a spectacular moment. When he finished the auditorium exploded. Now there was only one more song to go.

Clay, the most ambitious and astute of the final twelve, must have been in pieces. He knew Ruben had delivered a great performance. I knew he had chosen "Bridge Over Troubled Water" for his last song, and I also knew what a difficult song this is to sing. When Clay walked out onto the stage that night, I saw his nerves for the first time. For once, he seemed unsure. He closed his eyes and sang the first line. I could actually feel the hairs stand up on the back of my head. It was incredible. When he finished the audience went crazy. Clay looked triumphant. At that moment, I would have bet my house on Clay Aiken becoming the next American Idol.

I bumped into Ruben and Clay minutes afterward, just as we prepared for the media blitz. I looked at the two of them, and it was obvious that they both thought Clay had the victory sewn up. But at home later, watching the tapes, I changed my mind. Ruben's performance over the entire night was stronger. At any rate, it was too close to call.

The following day, as we were getting ready for the results show—a two-hour *American Idol* extravaganza—my house was total pandemonium. Phones were ringing off the hook, presents were arriving, people were running in and out. Terri was arranging everything; the whole world wanted tickets, and she ended up getting dressed in the limousine. At the theatre, it took about an hour to walk down the red carpet, and when I finally made it to the end, all I wanted to do was go to my dressing room. But when I asked the security guard, he had a funny look on his face. "You don't have a dressing room," he said. Neither did Randy or Paula. To say that I was furious was the understatement of the year. We had worked for months on this show, it was a big night for all of us, and we should have had a dressing room. Cue major tantrum.

FINAL JUDGMENT
The Best and Worst *American Idol* Performances

BEST

Tamyra Gray, "A House Is Not a Home." This was quite simply one of the best vocal performances I have ever heard. You have to remember that these contestants don't have the advantages of veteran stars, in equipment or backing musicians or proper rehearsal time. They don't have an awful lot of time to prepare the songs that week, and they're not as experienced. So when you get a standout performance like this, something on par with the best professional performances you have ever seen, it's just mind-blowing. It was really magical.

Kelly Clarkson, "Without You." In this case it wasn't on the actual show but the reprise the following night on the results show. A staggeringly good performance. That was the moment I felt that we had found a genuine star.

Clay Aiken, "Bridge Over Troubled Water." After some mistakes late in the competition, Clay almost pulled back even with Ruben as a result of this performance.

Clay Aiken, "Solitaire." Wonderful, sophisticated, subtle, and powerful. Interestingly, I haven't selected any of Ruben's performances because he was so consistent throughout. He always did an excellent job, but as a result, it's hard to say that any one stood out head and shoulders above the rest.

Kimberly Locke, "New York State of Mind." She often suffered because of her lack of personality, but she was technically the best singer of that second group, and this performance proved it.

WORST

Clay Aiken, "Grease." If I had been watching this on TV, I would actually have run out of the room. This is a perfect example of how a performer can go from amazing to awful. The red leather outfit, the ghastly winks, the horrible hip dance . . . to say it was dreadful is an understatement.

Ryan Starr, "You Really Got Me." A very close second to Clay's debacle. This is a girl who, if she were smart, could have become the next Britney Spears. She had some undefinable quality—she was actually gaining some momentum in the competition. I could see it when she took the stage. Then she made the mistake of trying to turn into a rock chick, and just murdered the song. Good-bye, Ryan.

Joshua Gracin, "Celebration." Awful. It was a musical nightmare. He had a cold, true, but in retrospect I wish it had been laryngitis.

Nikki McKibbin, "Ben." For that matter, just about any Nikki McKibbin performance, except that one week where she managed to squeak by Tamyra.

> **Jim Verraros, "Easy."** Jim was annoying simply because he
> was in the Top 10 and didn't deserve to be. I remember
> quite clearly sitting there miserably, thinking that it was one
> of the most terrible things I had ever witnessed.

Two of the producers, Charles and David, had thought it
would be a good idea for Paula and me to do some imaginary
love scene, because all season long the press had been speculating
about whether we were having an affair. Freedom of the press is
a good thing, but this seemed ridiculous. At any rate, we
thought it would be funny to do a scene shot at my house in
which Paula and I were having dinner. It would end with a kiss,
and then I would wake up, as if from a dream, to find Randy in
my bed—at which point I would scream. Wouldn't you? When
it was shown, however, it was far more graphic than I'd remembered. Paula was licking cream off her fingers in a very sexual
manner, and I was mortified. I looked behind me and caught
Terri's gaze. She wasn't amused.

Ryan was also mortified, but for different reasons. Every time
Ryan read out the number of total votes, or the vote differential,
he was depending on our backstage accountants to supply him
with the right information. But on this night the atmosphere
backstage was completely chaotic, and at one point he
announced that only about thirteen thousand votes had separated
the winner from the runner-up. A half hour later he retracted
that piece of information and said that in fact it had been even

closer, and that the margin had been only thirteen *hundred* votes. But as it turned out, the margin was more than a hundred and thirty thousand. Talk about a margin of error. Ryan got a pasting for that, but it wasn't his fault; he depended upon the numbers from the TelePrompTer, and they were wrong. So in the end, who came out on top? All of America knows, of course, but I will try to recapture it as I remember it.

On the night of the finale, as the results were about to be announced, the three judges were there behind our desk. Paula, Randy, and I were looking at one another, and back into the theatre, thinking of the two seasons we had been through together. It had been a draining experience, a consuming experience, and a wonderful experience. There was total silence in the auditorium as Ryan prepared to read off the winner. Was it Ruben? Was it Clay? Was it Ruben? Was it Clay? It was Ruben, and the entire theatre erupted in applause as Ruben stood there looking utterly stunned. Clay had a sort of fake smile on his face; he wasn't happy at all. The chaos consumed all of us. In fact, the only thing I remember clearly was Ruben and Clay leaving the auditorium on the way to the press tent. Ruben was surrounded by about two dozen people. He was sweating profusely and looked like he was on another planet. Clay, who came next, had one press representative. "My God," I thought, "there's the difference between being the winner and the runner-up."

As for Ryan, he nearly collapsed once the show was over. I had thought that might happen—he had been running on adrenaline for days, doing press appearances, sleeping infrequently if at

SIMON SAYS
What Will Become of the Season-Two Finalists

Vanessa Oliveris: Vanessa's appeal wasn't her voice; it was her wacky personality. She was a mixture of Bette Midler, Cyndi Lauper, and Betty Boop, and it would be very difficult for a record company to market her today. I think Vanessa could make a living in cabaret or maybe television—she was essentially a comedienne.

Charles Grigsby: The trouble with Charles was that he was forgettable. A very nice kid, with a nice voice—just nice. But nice doesn't make a star. There was nothing to root for. Nothing made him unique. There are thousands of Charleses in the world. He should use his status from *American Idol* to form a group; it is very unlikely he will succeed as a solo artist.

Julia DeMato: My advice to Julia would be to leave singing behind and go into acting. If they recast Joan Collins's role in *Dynasty*, Julia's the girl. The Julia I got to know but the public didn't was funny, sexy, and great fun to be around. Once again, her time on the show would open doors for her, but she should take acting lessons. If she really is determined to carry on singing, I think she may end up on a cruise ship.

Corey Clark: It's difficult for me to comment because of the circumstances behind his leaving the show. Corey was the rebel of the group. I found him to be charming, polite, and exactly the same offstage as he was onstage. Corey has an edge, and that is a good thing in the recording industry. I have a hunch that Corey could get himself a deal.

Rickey Smith: Rickey was the most popular *Idol* contestant to date. The judges loved him, the contestants loved him, the crew loved him. He was constantly asking me for advice offstage, but I just didn't know what to say to him. If I was really being honest, I would have told him to set his sights lower: Ricky, you will not be a star. You could, however, make a living from your voice. In truth, Rickey was a good amateur with a very likable personality. But I think he'll ultimately be remembered more for his "Hercules, Hercules" catchphrase than for his singing talent.

Kimberly Caldwell: A tricky one. Who is Kimberly? Is she a pop singer, a rock singer, or a Six Flags entertainer? I'm not sure and neither is she. All of the big stars in the world have an identity. That's why I struggled with her. She was quite good at most styles, but not great at anything. As I said before, she had been singing from the age of three. She was determined and confident but never gave a single standout performance. I know Randy is genuinely considering working with her. Who knows—if he finds her a great song, anything could happen. My opinion? I have a feeling that one day I may get off a roller coaster at an amusement park, hear someone singing in the background, and think, "I recognize that voice."

Carmen Rasmusen: Carmen, if she puts her mind to it, could achieve her dream. She has the potential to be a great country/pop artist. She's not the finished article—far from it. She needs to find a great vocal coach and work incredibly hard. But she has a fantastic tone to her voice, and if she finds a song like "Blue" or "Can't Find the Moonlight," she would have a hit. I liked Carmen a lot; she was sweet, enthusiastic, and most important she was never bitter. I really think she has a shot.

Trenyce: I find it hard to comment on Trenyce, because I can honestly say I know nothing more about her now than I did when she first auditioned. I don't know what she likes, or what she hates; I know she has a good voice, but that's it. The problem is that I think the American public felt the same way—which is extraordinary for someone who made the top twelve on one of the highest-rated shows in the U.S. In short, Trenyce lacked one vital factor: personality. Great voice, yes, but that's not enough. I believe that Trenyce will end up as a session singer, doing background vocals on someone else's records.

Joshua Gracin: I was a bit confused by Josh; I saw different sides to his personality throughout the competition. My first opinion was, he's the all-American boy: respectful, sincere, and I liked the fact that he was a Marine. At one point in the competition I actually thought he could win it. I later on saw a number of character flaws—he really couldn't take criticism. I actually think he wanted to punch me in the face. He had some good nights and some bad nights, and in truth the fact that he was a Marine helped him enormously. Once you took that away, there was nothing remarkable about him.

The future? If he is sincere about wanting to be a country music artist, he should pursue that. My advice—stay a Marine.

Kimberly Locke: As I've always said, she was technically the best singer in the competition. I think I was right when I said she was a bit boring. She was. America has always been the home of the best vocalists in the world: Go to any church across America and you will find great singers. And that's how I sort of felt about Kimberly—is there anything really different about you? The good news is that she has realized her dream. She got a recording deal with Curb Records after BMG decided not to offer her a contract. I really hope she does well. And you never know—she might.

Clay Aiken: I think Clay has changed *American Idol* forever—and I'm glad. Clay is the American dream. Six months ago he was a geeky-looking kid, working with underprivileged children, and singing for a hobby. Today Clay is probably the most talked about singer in America. He proved the point—you don't need to look like a male model to triumph in a contest like ours. Talent, personality, and determination will get you through. I confess that during season one, I had my own ideas about what the American Idol should look like. It wasn't Clay Aiken. I have always trusted the general public, and when we said, "What do you want?" in season two, they told us: Talent! Not hype. He is one of the best things to ever happen to *American Idol*—he broke the mold.

But Clay's success wasn't a fluke. He was determined, ambitious, and he thought through his choice of songs incredibly carefully. He knew (most weeks) what the audience wanted and he didn't disappoint. I think Clay can do whatever he wants in the future: sell records, act, or headline Vegas. I saw him two months after *American Idol* finshed. He hadn't changed. Thank God.

Ruben Studdard: Ruben won because he's a great singer. He was consistent and he had a smile that could light up an entire city. And once again, he was different. Who would have thought that someone weighing three hundred pounds would be *the* American Idol? Answer: America. I can't say a bad word about Ruben—what you saw on camera you saw offstage: a big guy with a big personality with a big voice. He was polite, humble, and understood that without this competition, he would never have gotten a recording contract.

I saw Ruben at the same time I saw Clay a few weeks ago. Once again, he hadn't changed. He still looked a little bemused by all the fuss. But he looked happy.

Both Ruben and Clay are in excellent hands. The famous Clive Davis is making their records. He adores both artists and is passionate about their music. The future for Ruben is bright—very bright indeed.

all. He was completely, utterly burned out. He never should have been hosting the results show, but he wasn't the kind of person to take a day off work—especially that day. And really, who could blame him? Everything we had worked for all season had culminated in a spectacular finish that not only drew tens of millions of viewers but would dominate all discussions of pop culture and the entertainment media for the foreseeable future.

So in the end, why did Ruben win? Well, first and foremost, he was a great singer. Secondly, he had a wonderful personality; he was, as Gladys Knight had observed, a velvet teddy bear that the public adored. Everyone wanted to support him. And also, even though he wasn't the best dancer, he had the indefinable X Factor. In terms of the vote, I think he also picked up Kimberly Locke's support when she was eliminated.

When Ruben won, Clay also lost, and I think there was a reason for that as well. Here was somebody who went all-out to win this competition, who prepared and prepared and thought and thought, who changed his image repeatedly to appeal more to the public. He wasn't so natural, but he was extremely good. Perhaps in the end, though, he overdid it to the point where he already looked like the finished article. Perhaps he didn't seem vulnerable enough.

At any rate, the vote was so close that Simon Fuller and I persuaded RCA to put the singles from both finalists out at the same time. They both were surprised, but once that plan was announced on live television, we had to follow through with it. I suppose that you could make an argument that it undermined Ruben's victory, but they were also, in a sense, co-champions, as the numbers had been so close. Ironically, when the singles were released, Clay's got to number one and Ruben's got to number two. This may have had something to do with the song choice: Clay had "Bridge Over Troubled Water" on his single and Ruben didn't.

The long-range development of Clay and Ruben, or for that matter Justin and Kelly, will be fascinating to watch. *American Idol* is like a laboratory of pop stardom. We have built the perfect beast, had our choice ratified by millions and millions of Americans, and then released that singer to the public. From here on, though, they will face all of the problems faced by any pop star: unpredictable shifts in the market or changes in the larger culture. What will happen to them? For once, your guess is as good as mine. The only piece of advice I gave to Kelly, Ruben, and Clay after the competition ended was to always remember who gave you this opportunity—the American public.

So You Wanna
Be a Pop Star

Believe it or not, I'm often approached by young singers
who ask me what they need to do to break into the music industry. I always start by giving people the same piece of advice:
Don't bother. Sometimes they laugh. Sometimes they shift
uncomfortably. But I'm dead serious. In almost every case,
"Don't bother" is the wise course. The odds of succeeding are
absolutely astronomical; in some ways, you would have better
luck if you set your heart on running a Fortune 500 company, or
ran for the U.S. Senate, or played the lottery. If you look around
and take the measure of every entertainer in every corner of the
country, I think you'll see what I mean. Have you ever met a

Simon's Top Five Classic Vocalists

- ★ Frank Sinatra
- ★ Bobby Darin
- ★ Tony Bennett
- ★ Bobby Hatfield of the Righteous Brothers
- ★ Ella Fitzgerald

hotel bar singer who tells you, "Yes, I entered the music business so I could end up singing in a hotel bar"?

But plenty of young singers don't listen to me when I tell them not to bother. They have drive and ambition, and they're convinced of their talent. Good for them. They have already passed the first test, which is to make sure that they have the stomach for this business. It's never an easy road, and even when you think you have made it, you can't rest. Any entertainment career requires ridiculous amounts of hard work and difficult sacrifices. Of course, the rewards, if you are lucky enough to enjoy them, are also large, but getting there is almost impossible.

Pop music is particularly tricky. I like to tell young singers that if they are geniuses who can write songs like Elton John or the Beatles, fantastic—you can rest easy. Anyone who can write "Sorry Seems to Be the Hardest Word" or "Eleanor Rigby" will draw the attention of one of the thousands of publishing companies out there. They'll snap you up within seconds. They are unique. But almost no one is as talented as Elton John or the Beatles. And if you're like most aspiring pop artists, you're primarily a performer. Pop acts are throwbacks in some ways; unlike modern rock bands, they tend not to write their own material. This means, of course, that a record company is investing in you as a performer, as a talent—they are banking that you have the charisma, the energy, the focus, and the X Factor to be able to sell millions of records. You are the musical equivalent of Leonardo DiCaprio: You're talented, but you need writers and direction.

This faith isn't free, though. If a record company signs you up as a solo artist and commits to a deal, they will have to invest millions of dollars in you. No company is going to do that unless they see something really special about you. And if the first single doesn't perform, the game may be over. The investment is gone. I'm not saying that this is an ideal circumstance, but it is reality. Trying to launch a solo artist who doesn't write his or her own material is the hardest thing in the world.

With that said, there are some basic rules that all aspiring singers and entertainers should follow. These don't guarantee you success, but they will help you maximize your chances, and that's all you can ask for. Because truthfully, even with my expert advice in hand, you're going to need all the help you can get.

Create a Platform

Pop artists don't appear out of thin air. Sometimes it seems like they do, but that's just skillful marketing and sleight of hand. The truth is that they all come from somewhere, and usually somewhere else within the entertainment industry. Without some preexisting context, in fact, they wouldn't have a chance in hell of being signed by any record company executive who wants to keep his job longer than a week or two. One way to establish yourself and create a platform, obviously, is to place yourself in a band. This is a bitter pill for many aspiring stars to swallow; most young entertainers have huge egos, and they all want to be the name above the title, the marquee star. But take it from me—it's nearly impossible to launch an unknown into a bona fide solo career. That's one of the reasons why *Pop Idol*, which turned into *American Idol*, was born. But there's an ironic by-product of the phenomenal successes. Because of Kelly and Justin and Ruben and Clay, there are tens of thousands of kids running around imagining that they can leap straight from their job as a cocktail waitress, or their position teaching children, to solo stardom. They can't. Why? Because Lionel Richie couldn't—he was in the Commodores before he enjoyed solo fame. And because Ricky Martin couldn't—he was in Menudo. And there are dozens of other examples, including:

★ Bobby Brown was in New Edition.

★ Beyoncé Knowles was in Destiny's Child.

★ Diana Ross was in the Supremes.

★ Annie Lennox was in the Eurythmics.

★ Björk was in the Sugarcubes.

★ George Michael was in Wham!

★ Robbie Williams, who is currently the biggest solo star in Europe, was previously in a group called Take That.

In fact, you can count the number of pop superstars who emerged fully formed as a solo artist on one hand: Elvis, Madonna, Prince, and precious few others. Throughout this book, I have used Justin Timberlake as an example of a present-day artist who correctly established himself long before his solo career even began. His main move, of course, was being in 'N Sync, although dating Britney Spears didn't hurt. If Justin Timberlake hadn't been in 'N Sync, no record company would have invested millions of its own money in him. He would have been an unknown with a nice enough personality, but without a great voice and without any known songwriting talent. For that matter, Michael Jackson, had he not been the lead singer of the Jackson Five, would never have become the most famous man on the planet. He first became a household name as the lead singer of a group, and without that group it's unlikely anyone would have taken a chance on him at fourteen, sixteen, or even eighteen. As immensely talented as he was, as ambitious as he was, he would have still been an unknown.

Another Jackson, Janet, followed a different course, but one that I also highly recommend—she began her career on television, with small roles on shows like *Good Times* and *Diff'rent Strokes* while she was still a little girl. This is an extremely wise

move, because it's founded on a sound business principle—
when you're starting off in an industry, you go where the work
is, and there are many more opportunities for small parts on
television than there are empty spots for artists at record labels.
In Janet Jackson's case, it paid off a decade later, when she
decided she wanted to be a pop singer. Since the road was
already paved, both by her family name and her TV career, she
had a smoother course on her way to stardom. The same thing
goes for Alanis Morissette, who knew that she wanted to be a
pop star when she was just a young girl. Rather than beat her
head against the door for years, she worked on a Canadian kids'
show, *You Can't Do That on Television,* for a few years, made a
name for herself, and then became a pop performer. (I have to
say that what Alanis achieved is close to a miracle. To me she is a
more successful illusionist than David Copperfield.) Britney
Spears and Christina Aguilera were in the Mickey Mouse Club.
Kylie Minogue was signed because she was already a big star on
an Australian soap opera, *Neighbors.* And that's how Natalie
Imbruglia got signed as well. Jennifer Lopez was a dancer on
In Living Color. For that matter, my own success with Robson
and Jerome proves this rule beyond any shadow of a doubt.
They were not singers. They were actors on a British television
show. That's how they were known and how they wanted to
be known. But when they had the opportunity to make pop
records, the public had no problem accepting them in their new
incarnation. My point is this: They were already entertainers,
and they had an existing platform. If you have the opportunity

to get a part on a television show, no matter how small it seems, take it. The chances are you won't be sorry.

I hope that what I'm communicating is that it's just as hard for the record labels as it is for the artists, but in a different way. They are operating under tremendous pressure to find and market the right stars, and they aren't willing to take risks. Since they'll be playing it safe, you have to put them at ease picking you. As somebody who gets paid a lot of money to find talent in pop music for an international label, I speak from experience—I am never just looking for a talent, but rather a talent with a head start. The business is too expensive now to just find somebody with a good voice and a good image, to mold them and refine them, and to then sit back and hope and pray that the public latches on. Trust me—the pop market is changing. When I look at any pool of people who are already in the entertainment industry, whether they're bit players on a TV show or a dance ensemble on a kids' show, I'm looking for future stars. If I spot one in that group, I know that I may be able to turn him or her into a breakout success. In other words, history will help you. Put yourself in the frame of mind of the record label: They're thinking, "Make my job easy for me!" To finally prove my point, who is number one on the charts at the time of this writing? Hilary Duff.

Use Your Connections

There are exceptions to these rules, of course, like Eminem, but that's just the result of utter genius sweetened by luck. His timing was immaculate, his songs are sensational, he has tabloid appeal, and he cuts across all races. And even Eminem, if you look more closely, had more than just his talent to recommend him: He came onto the scene closely associated with Dr. Dre, who was already an established producer. From the start, Eminem used his professional connections as well as his rivalries to elevate himself. A more recent example is 50 Cent, who was endorsed by both Eminem and Dr. Dre and became a huge star in his own right. The other good example of stardom by association was Whitney Houston, who was already known to people in the record industry because her mother was Cissy Houston, a session singer, and her aunt is Dionne Warwick. This was an accident of birth, and if you're not Dionne Warwick's niece, there's nothing you can do about it, but my point is that you need something that will help make you familiar to the record label when you first appear.

Find Good Material

Whether or not you're working with a record label, a pop star needs to have good songs. As a result, you need to find your way to the best songwriters and producers in the world. In simplistic terms, most good songwriters are whores. They go where the money is. And in any given year, you have somewhere between a half dozen and a dozen of what I would call grade-A pop songs. These are what I call career records, and they're songs like "Hit Me Baby One More Time" (by Britney Spears), "Beautiful" (Christina Aguilera), "Hero" (Enrique Iglesias), "Livin' La Vida

Loca" (Ricky Martin), "Vision of Love" (Mariah Carey), "Saving All My Love for You" (Whitney Houston), and so forth. Put yourself in the place of the people who are writing these kinds of songs. They don't come along very often. So why should you, as a writer, waste one of your grade-A songs on an unknown, when every artist and record label is lining up to record that material? If you give the song to the unknown, you may make him or her very happy, but you may not sell records. If you give the song to Christina Aguilera, you're guaranteed to sell three to six million albums worldwide. In the end, I tend to think it's the song that's more powerful than the performer, because I can think of at least a few cases where careers that were quite wounded were brought back to life by brilliant songs: Cher's "Believe" is one example; Kylie Minogue's "Can't Get You Out of My Head" is another. It's a catch-22 situation: Without the hit songs, artists don't have careers, but without careers, they're not going to have access to the hit songs. That's the brilliant stroke of *American Idol*—we are able to take these talented singers and pair them with material that even established artists would kill to record.

If that's the brilliance of *American Idol,* though, it's also the most obvious example of how the show creates an unreal world. To any singer who doesn't have access to a hit network television program as his or her launching pad, I would recommend finding your way to top producers and songwriters and attaching yourself to them in any way you can. You probably won't get their grade-A material, but if they like you and believe in your talent, you may get something—their grade-B material, or their grade-C material, or even their grade-D material. And anything from a top producer or songwriter is better than nothing; even if they just speak well of you in the industry, you'll be associated with their success. If, for example, as a new singer, you were able to get the Neptunes' writing and production team to agree to work with you, I guarantee that at least six major record labels would offer you a contract. And I know for a fact that songwriters and production teams, while they're not exactly easy to get in contact with, are easier to reach than the heads of record labels. Again, new artists need to be smart about their careers and take the path of lesser resistance when first establishing their names.

Get Representation

To get good material—or, for that matter, to get auditions— you're going to need someone to fight for you and champion you: In other words, you're going to need good representation. A singer with a credible agent looks more legitimate to the outside world, and he or she will obviously have an easier time getting in the door of a record label. Managers make things happen because they have track records, because they have the time to talk to many different labels, and because they have a history of success with those labels, and of course experience and expertise. And it is a talent, to be sure—I have dealt with many managers in my time, and it's hard to be tough on behalf of your client without alienating the companies that are footing the bill. Still, a good manager is an absolute necessity, because I have never, ever met anyone in my life who got a record deal by sending in an unsolicited tape. They don't get listened to—and if they do, the person who's doing the listening is a junior employee without any power to make a deal. In other words, it's a complete waste of time.

If a manager decides to take you on, it will be only because they think they can do some good for you, and you can do some good for them. Because of that, you should research your representation before seeking it out; certain managers specialize in certain kinds of acts. It's pointless going in to somebody who looks after rock bands if you want to be a pop star. Using normal channels—the Internet is probably your best bet—you should be able to do all the research you need in a few weeks, and that will help you get a tape to whoever you think might be a good manager. And remember, managers, while not exactly easy to get to, are easier to contact than some other people in the industry. Lou Pearlman, who put together 'N Sync and the Backstreet Boys, is more likely to take your call or listen to your tape than the head of BMG Records or Sony Records.

With that said, you should remember that managers need to be courted just like anyone else. When you send your package, make sure that everything about your presentation is professional and inviting. Good photos are something we always look for when we receive a package. Another thing that is quite important, though it may sound strange, is how the package is sealed and addressed: If it's written all in scribbles and bound up with acres of masking tape, it's likely to end up in the garbage.

By the same token, if you're able to set up a meeting with a prospective manager, act professional. One piece of important advice: Demonstrate that you know your business and that you can find a niche. (Is the biggest boy band in the world about to fall off in popularity? Is the top female solo star about to take a tumble? If so, then it's time to replace them, and any potential manager should know that you understand this.) Don't do the obvious—Manager: "Why are you here?" Singer: "Because I want to be famous." Follow the same rules, in short, that you would for an audition (see pages 225–28), because it *is* an audition. In a sense, it's the most important audition of your career.

Put in the Hard Work

American Idol comes at a strange time in the history of our pop culture. Today, kids are lazier than ever and more entitled. Often we have people who come in to see us in the auditions, people with good enough singing voices, and when we ask them if they have taken any lessons, they say no proudly. They shouldn't be proud. This isn't all about natural ability. In a way, being a pop singer is no different from being a great athlete. If you want to run the hundred-meters in ten seconds, you aren't going to do it without a coach. Many people start with talent, but you've got to train to hone your talent. If you're a runner, that means learning how to get off the blocks more quickly than anybody else and practicing until you perfect your form.

This has always been a problem on *American Idol,* particu-

larly in the first year. The contestants moaned
All I ever heard about was how tired they were.
didn't realize that singing was such hard work.
Clarkson complained. Generally, I have very littl
anybody who isn't prepared to put in fifteen-hou̲ ̲d̲a̲y̲s̲ ̲a̲t̲ ̲t̲h̲e̲
start of their career. While singing is hard work, it's not hard
labor: The contestants had to rehearse, do interviews, go
into studios, but generally they traveled in style, in luxury limousines that picked them up from their nine-room mansion in
Beverly Hills. Sometimes we would ask contestants why they
were on *American Idol,* and they would tell us that they had
prepared their whole life for this chance. Hearing that always
made me want to laugh. Their whole life? Give me a break.
These kids were nineteen years old. If you want a senior management position in a normal business, you can't expect to
get it in five seconds. You've got to work your way up. In my
case, I always knew I wanted to end up on top, but I never
assumed that it would be my next stop after the mailroom.
There's a myth in this business that if you don't hit by the time
you're twenty-five, you'll never make it. That's total rubbish. If
you look at some of the biggest artists in the world, some of
them are older—Sheryl Crow, for example, or Tina Turner, or
Cher. The biggest touring band in the world is still the Rolling
Stones, and they're not exactly spring chickens. No one is gov-
erned by age. Some of them kick around in the business for a
while before they get their break.

I think, strangely enough, that *American Idol* has magnified

FINAL JUDGMENT
The Best Pop Singles of All Time

Whitney Houston, "I Will Always Love You." This song showed her off perfectly. If you were going to rank a song and a vocal performance, you'd rank this a 10. You can't fault it.

The Righteous Brothers, "Unchained Melody." This song has something really unique about it—it is almost impossible to get tired of it. The structure is part of the reason; it's not organized like a traditional song, which is why it's called "Unchained Melody." But it also has this amazing ability to sell emotion. If it's used in the right context, it's the saddest and most beautiful song in the world. I have had a number of artists record it, and every time it has sold over a million copies. If I found the right singer, I would do it again.

Diana Ross, "Ain't No Mountain High Enough." The original is superb, and there are many other versions that are also good. Wonderful.

Britney Spears, "Hit Me Baby One More Time." If you ever had to define the perfect pop single, this is it. It's more than a hit single—it's a career song.

Elvis Presley, "Suspicious Minds." Perfection.

The Beatles, "She Loves You." This song changed the sound of pop music forever.

the entitlement problem. It shows these young singers enjoyi.. what is, essentially, impossible success, and so many viewers start to feel as though they, too, will be plucked from obscurity. That's just as crazy as thinking that you're going to win the lottery. Even on the show I have seen this problem. In either season, it was clear from the first or second week who the finalists would be. There were some performers who, try as they might, were never going to make it into the top three. Part of my job, I always felt, was to tell them that. If I let Nikki McKibbin entertain for one moment the thought that she might win, I would have been fueling her delusion. If I let Kimberly Caldwell go on thinking she was going to be the next American Idol, I would have been lying to her. Instead, I wanted to prick the bubble of this self-absorbed egotism. This isn't to say that those two girls— or any other contestant—can't make it eventually, only that they have lots of work ahead of them. When singers get voted off *American Idol*, many of them feel that their apprenticeship in the entertainment industry has ended, and they wind up at home, sitting by the phone, waiting for a call from a record executive. That's ridiculous. The truth, of course, is that their apprenticeships have just begun. They have a head start because they have been on national television, and they should use that to their advantage, but their careers are still in their infancy. And without continued effort and hard work, they will go nowhere.

Reaching the
Finish Line

Once you decide to devote yourself to a pop career, you're going to spend much of your time in audition rooms. If you were a lawyer, you'd spend your time in court. If you were a surgeon, you'd spend your time in the operating room. As *American Idol* proves, audition rooms are where entertainment careers are born—or die a premature death. It's vital to know how to handle the audition process. And while I have spent the last two years watching people walk through the *American Idol* rooms, I have spent the last twenty-five years in the business. Here are my top ten tips for auditions. Oh and by the way, this is assuming you can sing in tune.

1. **Don't copy another performer.** I'd say that 90 percent of the people who come to our auditions, no matter how talented they are, have perfected only the art of mimicry. They have listened to an artist they like countless times—Alicia Keys is probably the most common model at the moment—and they are certain that they can succeed by copying a success. But what we're looking for is somebody original. The biggest stars you can think of, and the most enduring, may be similar to other stars, but they are still unquestionably unique. There is only one Elton John. There is only one Madonna. There is only one Cher. There was only one Frank Sinatra. And there is only one Michael Jackson, thank God.

2. **Don't overstyle yourself.** You see this all the time. My interpretation of somebody who overdresses for an audition is that they're desperate. What we're looking for is people who are comfortable in their own skin, and when we see people come in with hats, things around their wrists, one trouser leg tucked carefully into a boot, it just looks like a gimmick. I don't believe in underdressing—I think you've got to look as if you're serious—but this overdetermined-pop-star look is absolutely loathsome. Sunglasses are the worst.

3. **Don't sing and dance at the same time.** First of all, it smacks of cabaret. And also, it's very difficult to dance when you're singing without a backing track. You'll likely run out of

I DON'T MEAN TO BE RUDE, BUT . . .
I Hate Pop-Star Clothes

When we started *American Idol*, many contestants came to auditions in what I called their pop-star clothes. They were hideous: girls auditioning in sunglasses, hats, leather, thigh-high boots, etc., or guys trying to show off their bodies by keeping their shirts open. I don't blame the individuals entirely. In 2003, there's probably less of an image in pop music than there ever used to be. If you look back to the sixties, the Beatles created their own particular look with suits and haircuts—and then evolved that look over the years. In the seventies, there was glam rock and punk rock; in the eighties, we had the New Romantics; in the nineties, we had grunge. But that was the beginning of the end, in a sense, because the absence of style was considered a viable style. Today, it's very difficult to pinpoint the proper image for a pop star. There are two people who have got it right at the moment: Avril Lavigne and Pink. They're both cool and accessible. But more important, teenage girls can relate to what they're wearing.

breath. I always advise against singing and dancing. Some of the worst auditions we've seen on *American Idol* are the singer/dancers. Remember Keith?

4. **Make eye contact when performing.** This is a sign of comfort and confidence. When you're doing an audition and you're

gazing up to the ceiling, it's very difficult for us to know what's going on in your head. You seem nervous and unsure of yourself. It's a simple, small thing, but very important.

5. **Choose the right song for your personality.** I can't stress this enough: There are songs that are right for your voice and your personality, and songs that are wrong. One of the most off-putting things we see when we're on the road is a sixteen-year-old girl who walks in, looks very hip, and then sings a Patsy Cline song. To me that doesn't make sense.

6. **Don't grovel when you come in.** Again, I look upon it as an act of desperation. So many times people come in and they come up with this terrible dialogue about how much they like me or Randy or Paula. It's demeaning, and there's no point to it. We're not looking to find a nice person; we're looking for somebody who's confident and assured, but talented above all. Trust me—most stars aren't nice.

7. **Believe in yourself the second you leave the house.** Self-possession isn't something you can turn on seconds before you walk into the audition room. People like Ruben or Kelly or Frenchie believed in themselves from the minute they woke up in the morning. If you try to cobble it together in the waiting room, you'll fail.

8. **Be sure to eat and drink prior to an audition.** Food is fuel, and you don't want to run out of fuel. Over and over again, I have seen

people forget the words, or start to get emotional. When I ask them when they last ate, and they say, "Twenty-four hours ago," I lose my patience. This sounds like silly advice, but it's important. Also, staying hydrated is essential for your throat.

9. **Rehearse.** When Michael Jackson was asked the three most important things for aspiring stars, he said, "Rehearse, rehearse, rehearse." You need to know your material well enough that it's second nature. If you have to try to remember the lyrics, you'll lose your confidence.

10. **Listen.** Sometimes a judge or a talent executive will see something in you but want you to try something slightly different. Sometimes they'll want you to try something entirely different. When I say to a contestant, "You're not picking the right material for your voice," or "You need to take dancing lessons," or "Your hair looks awful," I'm not saying it because I like to be critical—or rather, I'm not saying it only because I like to be critical. I'm saying it because it's true. Be receptive to suggestions, and recognize that someone with experience in the music business might be able to see something in you that you don't see in yourself. In other words, stop sulking.

Embracing Celebrity

Let's say that you're lucky enough to get to the second stage in your career, that as a result of your perseverance, your connections, and/or your wonderful auditions, you have joined a band or landed a small role on a television show. Now you need to take it one stage further. So what do you do? Easy: Date a celebrity.

Elizabeth Hurley is now one of the most famous people on the planet. How did she get famous? She dated Hugh Grant. Of course, while she was dating Hugh Grant, she turned up for a premiere in a Versace dress that was literally put together with safety pins. But the fact that she was with Hugh Grant, the fact that she was his girlfriend, got her photographed in every newspaper in the world. For a while there, she was the name in bold next to his, the name that readers didn't quite know but that they knew they should know. That was an incredibly effective way of launching a career.

Pardon me for being cynical, but I believe that many celebrity couples are complete PR illusions. Sometimes relationships between stars are genuine, but just as often they are skillful ways of getting a relative unknown into the spotlight. When you're an aspiring celebrity and you pair off with another aspiring celebrity, you don't just double or triple your exposure. Rather, you multiply it by a factor of ten or twenty. People in the media are fascinated, and always have been, by the idea that famous or even semifamous people are shagging each other. Look at how many stars change mates just before the opening of a new film, or before the release of a new album. P. Diddy said something a little while ago that got him ridiculed in the press— he said that he pioneered the trend of celebrities dating celebrities. But in a way, he's right. When he had his relationship with

J.Lo, both of their careers went through the roof afterward. J.Lo learned this lesson well—her relationship with Ben Affleck, while it may well have had something to it, was also a canny PR move, *Gigli* notwithstanding. The same thing goes for Beyoncé and Jay-Z; it's one of the least likely pairings on earth, but tabloids love to write about it and speculate. And then, of course, Demi Moore and Ashton Kutcher: Add one not-very-respected young actor and one not-so-remembered aging actress, and what do you have? The top entertainment story of the year.

You may think I'm joking, but I'm completely serious. Entertainment careers are all about momentum and coverage, and relationships are an important part of that. And remember, celebrity relationships don't even have to be normal. Take Michael Jackson and Lisa Marie Presley. Were those two people genuinely in love? Of course they were. NOT. I believe it was a pact to ensure further fame for both of them—just as it was when Lisa Marie went on to marry the actor and well-known Elvis fan Nicolas Cage. If Ricky Martin ever bothered to give me a call and ask my advice, I'd tell him to snap up a celebrity girl-friend—quick!

The same goes for someone like Mariah Carey—poor old Mariah, desperately hunting through the racks at the celebrity store, looking for a proper boyfriend. There were rumors that she was dating Eminem, which she then came out and denied, but the rumors did their job for a little while.

SIMON AS CUPID
Predictions for Today's Top Celebrity Couples

Brad Pitt and Jennifer Aniston: True love.

Ashton Kutcher and Demi Moore: Won't last a year.

Jay-Z and Beyoncé: Dubious.

Ben Affleck and J.Lo: Won't last a year.*

David Beckham and Victoria Beckham: True love.

Justin Timberlake and Cameron Diaz: Very dubious.

Guy Ritchie and Madonna: True love.

Paul McCartney and Heather Mills: True love.

Michael Jackson and anyone: A complete sham.

P. Diddy and himself: True love.

*In the two days since I compiled this list, Affleck and J.Lo have broken off their engagement—for the first time, anyway. Because of printing deadlines, other couples may no longer be intact by the time this book arrives in bookstores. But don't worry—after celebrities split up, they just turn around and date other celebrities!

Staying on Top

Once you have made it to the top—wherever your particular top may be—maintaining your fame is extremely tricky. Many stars fall from their perch so rapidly that they lose their dignity along with their reputation. Take Prince, for example. For a time, he was arguably one of the most famous people on the planet. He could do no wrong. He was selling tens of millions of records a year, filling stadiums, making movies, and then at some point it just stopped. As an outsider, it seemed to me that he had ceased to reside in reality, that he had lost touch with all aspects of his artistry and career. That general piece of advice—don't lose touch—is getting harder and harder as the pop-culture climate distorts fame and breeds a certain sense of entitlement. Here are some other important points to remember:

* **Don't lose touch with reality.** I quite like Mariah Carey, and I had the opportunity to spend some time with her in the studio, but I can honestly say it was one of the weirdest experiences of my life. During the entire afternoon I spent with her, there was only one subject that she could talk about: herself. It was also the only subject her entourage could talk about. At the time, she was beginning a period of decline in her career, but you would never have known it from the people around her. They agreed with her on everything, whether it was her publicists or makeup people or backing singers. In this particular case, we met because she had produced and

sung a duet with one of my artists, Westlife. When the tape was sent to me, I played it and I was absolutely horrified. It was terrible. I phoned her record company in London to tell them that I wasn't putting the record out. They fought, but I held my ground. Finally, they asked whether I would tell Mariah myself, and I said that I would be happy to. That's why I had to fly to Canada to meet her and, in the midst of her "yes" brigade, tell her that I thought the production was horrendous and needed to be changed before the record could be released. When I said as much, there was a deadly silence; it was as if I had spit on the Queen in court. But I couldn't care less. I just wanted a hit. In the end, we did change the record, and it went to number one. I have to say that I love Mariah—she is a genuine star and ironically her diva-ness is part of her appeal. But I wasn't surprised when her career went downhill: It was clear that she had no one around her to tell her the truth. Prince was probably in a similar situation, and it cost him dearly—I don't think he has put out a decent record in ten years.

★ **Don't make any sudden moves.** Stars like Elvis Presley and Frank Sinatra understood—or their management understood—what got them to the top. Most notably, they understood the value of working with great songwriters, and there was a trust between artist and management that endured. But many pop stars let their fame go to their head, and at some point they decide that they want to write their own songs. The rationales are insane: They want to "move on," or "change their audience." Well, it's risky, certainly, in pop music. Kylie Minogue, after five years in the wilderness, after putting out two disastrous indie rock albums that she felt better expressed her personality as an artist, came back to pop music with one of the strongest records of all time, "Can't Get You Out of My Head," and revived her international stardom. She didn't change her audience. She changed *back* to her original audience.

★ **Don't start believing in your own genius.** One of the best examples of career meltdown was an artist called Terence Trent D'Arby. He was a British singer—American-born, actually—who had played around Europe, and he surfaced in the late eighties with one of the best debuts I have ever heard. It was sensational. He had a fantastic soul voice, lots of style, and he even wrote his own material. It didn't seem like there was any chance that he would fail. Around that time, I bumped into him, and to say his head was up his own ass would have been the understatement of the year. He was arrogant, disconnected, and he seemed unfocused on everything but his own ego. People always say that success has changed this artist, or that one, but I find that success rarely changes anyone. Rather, it gives them the power to be what they always were—assholes. Terence Trent D'Arby went on like this, suddenly unconstrained by propriety, and when his second album came out, it was an all-time turkey. I have spoken with people who worked with him on that record, and evidently he had lost all sense of reality. He considered himself to be a god, some kind of infallible creative genius, and he wouldn't listen to any criticism. Well, he should have, because that second record killed his career. Recently, I saw that he has resurfaced with a new name—he's Sananda something-or-other—and a new record. He may creep back into people's consciousness, but he's nothing compared to what he could have been. Pop stars also have this funny career disease in which they begin to believe that they can write or cowrite their songs. It's almost an unwritten rule that by the second or third album there are cowriting credits. It is my belief that writing a hit song is one of the hardest jobs on earth. And yet everyone believes they can do it. To my mind, this is rubbish. Can you imagine creating a new sitcom, hiring actors, and then after a breakout year having the actors insist on writing scripts and directing? It happens in some cases eventually, but nowhere near as quickly. Television stars accept that they're being highly paid for following someone else's direction and script. Pop stars have a problem with it. From a label's perspective, if you can find an artist who is a gifted songwriter—hallelujah! Those people are so rare that they're like the Loch Ness monster. If one appears, get a photograph to prove that he or she exists.

★ **Don't think you can go it alone.** Artists also let their egos destroy their relationships with their mentors, and that's a fatal error. Many artists are young. They are talented but inexperienced, and they desperately need people to tell them which way is up. One of the best mentors in this business is Clive Davis, who was the head of Arista Records and now runs RCA/J Records. He is in his early seventies, and as a result he knows about a thousand times more than an eighteen-year-old kid. It's true that pop music is a youth market, but it's also a business. Clive usually attaches himself to artists early on, and those artists tend to remain viable for many years. He was a mentor for Whitney Houston, for Carlos Santana, for so many others. If they have listened to him, they have increased their chances of survival. Similarly, my friend Simon Fuller managed the Spice Girls. After two successful albums they fired him because they thought they knew better. Goodbye, Spice Girls.

★ **Don't pay too little attention to what people say about you.** This is especially true of the *American Idol* singers, and I used to tell them this all the time. I told Kelly. I told Justin. I told Ruben. I told Clay. I explained that they were all in a unique position in the entertainment industry, because they were effectively the people's champions. Ordinary Americans were asked to give their opinion on who was the most entertaining, or the most talented, or the most compelling, and they voted for you. They created you. And quite literally, without them you're nothing. If you drift too far away from that anchor, if you forget about the people who put you on the top, you'll become unglued. So any day, at any time, if any-one asks for your autograph or wants to shake your hand, don't turn away. Instead, remember how much you relied on these people. A few months after the second season ended, I bumped into Ruben and Clay at a *Vanity Fair* photo shoot, and I was pleasantly surprised. They weren't on star trips. They had retained their enthusiasm. They were pleased to see me. I think in those two cases they just happen to be wonderfully nice people. Maybe audiences picked up on that, and that's part of the reason they made it as far as they did. Whatever the reason, I hope they continue on just as they've been going.

★ **Don't stop working.** The artists who endure are the ones who stay focused even after they have reached the top of their profession. I saw it with Madonna. I see it with Beyoncé. I see it with J.Lo. I used to see it with Michael Jackson. Remember, in this business there's always someone younger and hungrier coming up behind you.

Since we have spoken about the artists who have bombed spectacularly after huge success, we should also look at some artists who've had enduring popularity. Barbra Streisand can be out of the news for five years, but if she announced tomorrow that she was holding a concert, it would probably sell out faster than any concert on earth. She is like one of those movie stars from the forties—she lives in the mansion on the hill, the public knows a little bit about her private life, but she's not plastered all over the tabloids every day. In fact, she's almost the opposite of Madonna—while Madonna gives it all away in each incarnation and then has to remake herself to replenish her mystique, Barbra Streisand keeps her distance, is a little cooler, but is no less respected. Of the newer crop, I think that Justin Timberlake really is a force to be reckoned with. Whether he was advised to plan his career the way he did, or whether he instinctively knew how, he understood the point of springboard appeal. He started in 'N Sync, as Britney Spears's boyfriend, and he has evolved into a full-fledged star. Beyoncé has also done everything right up to this point: She began in Destiny's Child, has done some acting to establish herself as more than a singer, and has a high-profile relationship with another entertainer. She seems entirely determined to stay on top and, in time, become one of the great pop stars. And Jennifer Lopez has that same ultimate determination that has defined many of pop's biggest names. She will go to any length to stay in the public eye, and her quality control is incredible. Those are the people who I really believe are special. They are not necessarily the best singers around. But look in their eyes and you will see a real determination and hunger. What links all of these artists: Ambition with a capital "A."

American Idol has run for two years, garnering huge audiences and launching the careers of some of the most exciting young singers in the world. I was there at the beginning, and I was

I DON'T MEAN TO BE RUDE, BUT . . .
George Michael Committed Career Suicide

If ten years ago you had told people that George Michael's career would be in jeopardy in 2003, they would have looked at you like you were crazy. He has had trouble with record labels, personal struggles, and so forth. But he still had a chance. He even had a chance after he made Universal spend an outlandish amount of money on his "Freeek!" single, and it stiffed. He was trying to act hip, when in fact he had matured quite a bit from his Wham! days. That didn't help him, but what really killed him was when he went out with his next single, "Shoot the Dog," and attacked the United States. America is a very proud nation that was at a vulnerable point in its history, and here was a guy who had made tens of millions of dollars from its citizens, and he was going on record attacking them. It was disrespectful and stupid. If he asked for my advice, not that he would in a million years, I would tell him that his career is singing ballads and mid-tempo records. Quite simply, that's what he does best.

there in the middle, and I may well be there at the end, whenever that is. If I had to distill one lesson from this entire process—and from the two decades I spent in the record business before *American Idol* was a gleam in anyone's eye—it would be that entertainers do not rise to the top of their craft, or even to the middle, without determination. Determination is an overused word, and the idea has become something of a cliché, but it's vital and it's true. In my career I've had thirty-four number-one singles. I've sold over ninety million records. I have broken all sorts of world records for artists having the most consecutive number-one singles, but when I was starting off, it didn't come easily to me. When I eventually got the job I wanted, I was told many, many times that what I was doing wasn't good enough. I was never happy about it, but there was something in the back of my mind that told me that my critics were right, and not particularly malicious, and I resolved to get better so that I could create the proper opportunities for myself. And I did.

There must be hundreds if not thousands of people today singing in hotel bars and local bands who are great singers. Talented, attractive, charismatic—the whole package. But they don't have the determination to take it further. They have reached their comfort zone. If Madonna wasn't Madonna and you found her in the Holiday Inn in Detroit singing "Evergreen," you wouldn't necessarily think of her as a woman who could be the biggest recording artist in the world. It was her determination and confidence that turned her into a star, her idea of herself as superior that separated her from the rest of the pack. When people get turned down by us on *American Idol,* some of them look deflated, like it's the end of the world. I would like to see some of them resurface a year later, or three years later, with a new image, a better sense of their talent, and a career. It would be inspiring to me if some of the *American Idol* losers became stars of the same magnitude as the winners. It would speak to their focus and ambition. It would prove many different wonderful things about the record industry, all at once.

To be a recording artist selling records around the world is probably the best job anyone could ever hope to have. The business is unpredictable and ruthless, but the rewards are potentially huge. And what makes it all so wonderful is—it could be you.

Acknowledgments

The day after the second *American Idol* season finale, I was exhausted. It wasn't just that the show was over—six months of hard work had ended and I was drained. Interestingly, one thought came into my mind: how important the entire team was to the success of the show. I was literally a cog in the wheel—it sounds like a cliché to say it was a team effort, but it was. So many people and companies contributed, and since this is my book I would like to feature some of them:

Simon Fuller. Simon was the captain of the ship. A quiet, determined man, he had made millions from television and music, and had a point to prove. He wanted to make the most spectacular show on earth—and he did. Years ago he said to me that if we ever worked together, we'd have the biggest artist in the world. Put the *Idol* artists' sales together from around the globe and we accomplished just that. Simon was the strategist who couldn't take no for an answer. He believed in the show's chances of success in America more than anyone else, and his relentless push made it happen. Many people said that it was going to be impossible for the two of us to work together without killing each other. We're both still alive and have become good friends.

Sandy Grushmaw, Gail Berman, Mike Darnell—the famous three from the Fox network. I got to know them all well during the second season and would see Mike two or three times a week along with his adorable wife who never leaves his side. Gail Berman is a very special person and a very smart girl; I have already made up my mind that she will be the one to teach me about television drama. And Sandy and his boss, Peter Chernin, have truly impressed me with their long-range plan for the show; it was because of them and their incredible commitment that I've signed a long-term deal with *American Idol.* Working with Fox has been a total pleasure. These guys are relentless, and what I admire most about them is the support and confidence they gave to the British producers. They broke just about every rule on American TV and succeeded. Success is hardly ever a fluke, and they deserve every bit they have achieved. They contributed a hell of a lot of character to the show and made it the best *Idol* show in the world.

Nigel Lythgoe, Kenny Warwick, Cecil Frot-Coutaz. Nigel and Kenny are the British executive producers on the show, and they are the Steven Spielberg of television. Most of the humor and the edge come from these two, and their attention to detail is second to none. And I believe they do such a great job because they truly love the show. And Cecil is the Unsung Hero, working behind the scenes for Freemantle in the United States—she has been a rock. She is also one of the most instinctive people I have ever met.

BMG. I have worked for BMG for fourteen years, and what makes them special is that they never second-guess you, and they allow you to be an entrepreneur. I don't believe many companies would have allowed me to judge this show all over the world. The new regime there is the best I have ever worked with, and I am extremely grateful for all the support they have given me. And Sonny, who runs my label for me in the U.K., has proven how right I was to hire him.

Clive Davis. Thank God for Clive Davis. He took over the project in the United States and he made the dream a reality. He also made the artists credible. He has a great team, including Steve Ferrara, Richard Sanders, and Charles Goldstuck. If I can achieve one-tenth of what Clive has achieved in my life, I'll be a very happy person.

Alan Berger of CAA. CAA have been incredibly supportive, and I'm very grateful for everything that Alan and his staff have done for me since I arrived in America. Alan is a class act.

And lastly, no book would be complete without thanks to those who made it happen: my brother Tony Cowell, Luke Janklow of Janklow & Nesbit, Ann Campbell and the rest of the team at Broadway Books, and Ben Greenman. The problem with acknowledgments, of course, is that you leave people out. If I have forgotten you, I apologize; the book would have been huge. I suppose what I am trying to say to all of these people and companies is—thank you.

W?